M3 Gun Motor Carriage

Written by David Doyle

Detail In Action®

AF597279

Cover Art by Don Greer

Squadron/Signal Publications

(Front Cover) In the thick of the fighting on Iwo Jima on 11 March 1945, an M3 Gun Motor Carriage, also known to the Marines as a Self Propelled Mount (SPM), opens fire on Japanese positions.

(Back Cover) Even after the U.S. Army replaced the M3 with more powerful, fully tracked vehicles, the Gun Motor Carriages fought on. Many were transferred to the British Commonwealth, which used the vehicles, like this one, as self-propelled artillery in Italy.

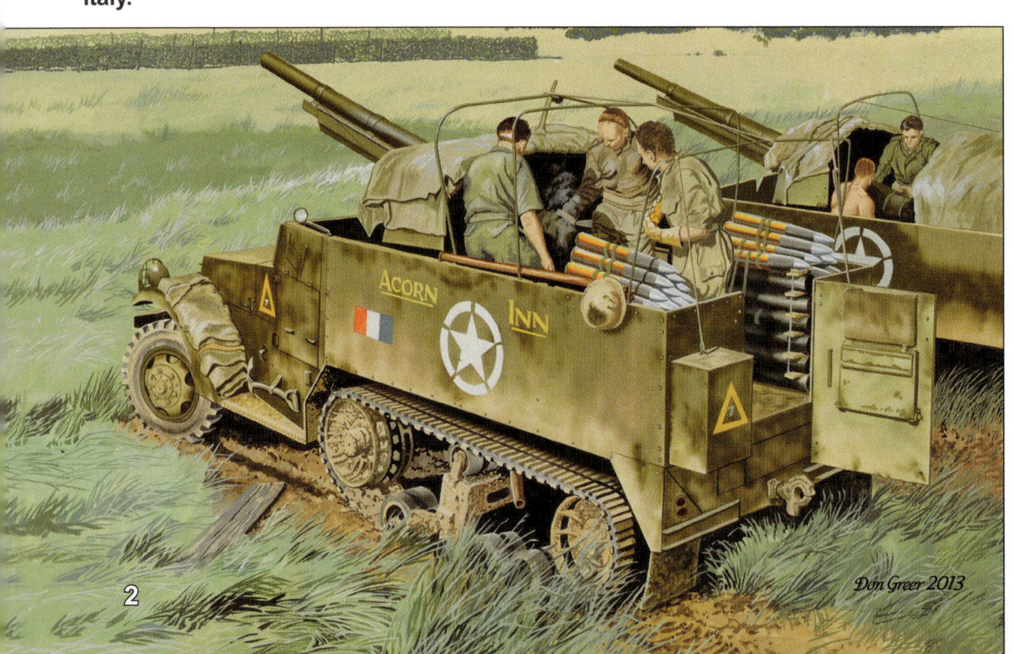

About the Detail In Action® Series

Detail In Action books trace the development of a single type of aircraft, armored vehicle, or ship from prototype to use. The equipment is shown in action and then specific close-up details of important sections of the equipment are explained. Experimental or "one-off" variants can also be included. Our first *In Action*® book was printed in 1971.

Squadron/Signal Walk Around® books feature the best surviving and restored historic aircraft and vehicles. Inevitably, the requirements of preservation, restoration, exhibit, and continued use may affect these examples in some details of paint and equipment. Authors strive to highlight any feature that departs from original specifications.

Hardcover ISBN 978-0-89747-727-7
Softcover ISBN 978-0-89747-728-4

Proudly printed in the U.S.A.
Copyright 2013 Squadron/Signal Publications
1115 Crowley Drive, Carrollton, TX 75006-1312 U.S.A.
www.SquadronSignalPublications.com

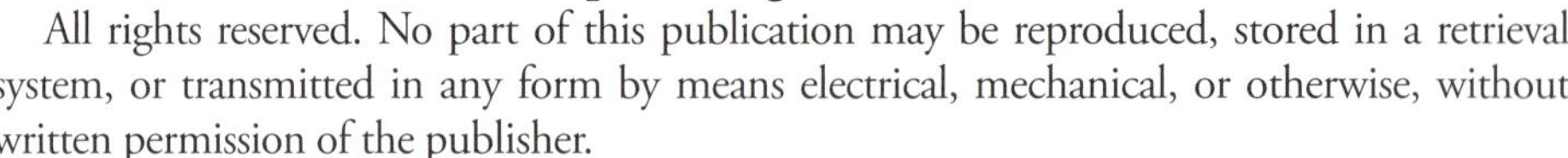

All rights reserved. No part of this publication may be reproduced, stored in a retrieval system, or transmitted in any form by means electrical, mechanical, or otherwise, without written permission of the publisher.

Military/Combat Photographs and Snapshots

If you have any photos of aircraft, armor, soldiers, or ships of any nation, particularly wartime snapshots, please share them with us and help make Squadron/Signal's books all the more interesting and complete in the future. Any photograph sent to us will be copied and returned. Electronic images are preferred. The donor will be fully credited for any photos used. Please send them to the address above.

(Title Page) A column of Marine M3 75mm SPMs heads to the front during the battle for Saipan Island. The interior of the M3 became quite crowded in actions like these, often with extra ammunition packed in every available space. These crews have hung some of their personal gear on the outside of the vehicle, where it swings from bars that have been added in the field, apparently for this purpose. (National Archives)

Dedication

Dedicated to the late Dave Harper, who inherited his passion for the Marine Corps, and all things related to the Corps, from his father. David began the project that became this book, but regrettably was not able to see it to completion.

Introduction

As German Panzers rolled across Europe, it became evident that the U.S. badly needed a mobile, effective antitank weapon. Beginning in June 1941, a team led by Major Robert Icks started to develop such a vehicle based on an M3 halftrack personnel carrier. Initially designated the T12, the Gun Motor Carriage consisted of a M1897A4 75mm gun, often referred to as a "French 75," mounted on the halftrack from which it could be fired. Later, Icks would become a pioneer researcher into the history of armored fighting vehicles.

To create the T12, the M3's glass windshield was removed, and the windshield armor modified to hinge down rather than the normal up. It was also notched to clear the barrel when the cannon was in the traveling position. The fuel tanks were relocated to the rear of the vehicle and the seats and subfloor of the M3 were eliminated and replaced with a subfloor with 10 four-round ammo stowage compartments for the 75mm weapon.

After initial testing of the pilot vehicle, an additional 36 of these new tank destroyers were built in August and September of 1941 and were tested at Aberdeen Proving Ground and by the 93rd Antitank Battalion at Fort Meade, Maryland. A further 50 T12 vehicles were produced and rushed to the Philippines before the end of 1941.

On 30 October 1941 the T12 was standardized as the 75mm Gun Motor Carriage M3 and the first production contract, number W-670-ORD-1765, for 1,350 vehicles was issued to the Autocar Company. Production began in February 1942, and all were delivered by the end of the year. This was followed by contract W-670-ORD-2597, initially for 626 vehicles, and later extended by 30 more, which were completed in 1943.

Autocar assigned serial numbers 87 through 1436 to the vehicles on the first contract, to which the Army assigned registration numbers 4017060 to 4018409. The next block of serial numbers, 1437 to 1466, carried registration numbers 4053350 to 4053379, and serial numbers 1467 to 2092 bore registration numbers 4053724 to 4054349.

Great Britain received a number of these vehicles. Because demand for the new vehicle exceeded the number of M2A3 gun carriages available for creating the 75mm Gun Mount M3, a change to the M2A2 carriage brought about a new classification of M3A1 Gun Motor Carriage in July 1942. The gun mount itself based on the M2A2 was the M5.

However, as more effective tank destroyers began pouring from America's factories, the shortcomings of the halftrack-based tank destroyers – specifically in protection, mobility, and firepower – became apparent. Therefore, late in 1943 Autocar was issued contract 26-034-1417 to convert 113 of the vehicles into M3A1 Halftrack Personnel Carriers. Once converted, these vehicles bore manufacturer's serial numbers 40128 through 40240.

For the same reason – that is, by being eclipsed by better vehicles – the M3 and M3A1 Gun Motor Carriages were reclassified as Limited Standard in March 1944. In August 1944 the classification was changed again to Obsolete. Yet another conversion contract was issued to Autocar, 36-34-1878, calling for 1247 of the M3 Gun Motor Carriages to be rebuilt into additional M3A1 personnel carriers. Once converted, these vehicles received new serial numbers 47636 through 48882. The vehicles kept their original registration numbers. While in essence discarded by the U.S. Army, other forces, the British, and the U.S. Marines, continued to use the M3 to considerable advantage well into 1945.

The main weapon of the 75mm GMC M3 was the 75mm Gun M1897A4 on a modified Carriage M2A3. This piece was an improved version of the French 75mm Gun M1897, which was used extensively by the French and Americans in World War I. (Patton Museum)

Acknowledgments

This book would not have been possible without the help of a number of enthusiasts and historians, among them Dave Harper, Tom Kailbourn, the staffs of the National Museum of the Marine Corps and National Archives, as well as the Patton Museum. Brent Mullins not only completed an outstanding restoration of a scarce M3 Gun Motor Carriage, but was also gracious enough to allow me and Dave Harper to climb over, under, and through it, taking photos. As always, my wife Denise worked beside me, doing research and helping with photography, and for that and many other things I am supremely grateful.

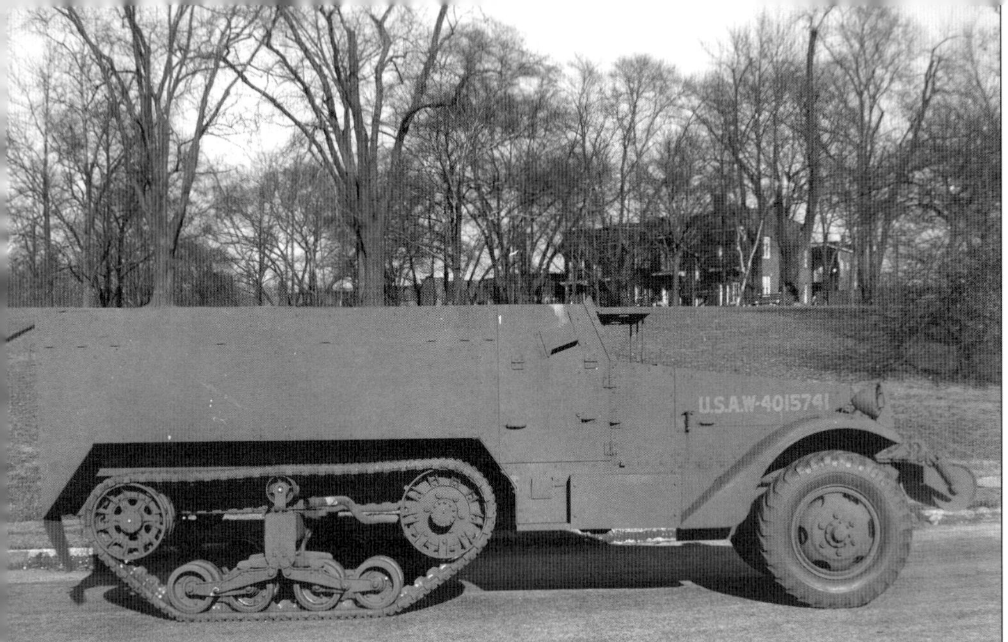

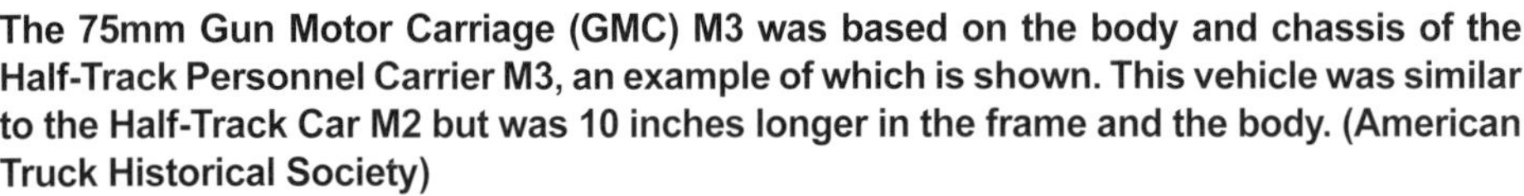

The 75mm Gun Motor Carriage (GMC) M3 was based on the body and chassis of the Half-Track Personnel Carrier M3, an example of which is shown. This vehicle was similar to the Half-Track Car M2 but was 10 inches longer in the frame and the body. (American Truck Historical Society)

A Half-Track Personnel Carrier M3 chassis is viewed from the rear. The frame consisted of longitudinal channels reinforced and braced with pressed-steel cross sections. For the conversion to the 75mm GMC M3, the frame would be strengthened. (American Truck Historical Society)

Powering the Half-Track Personnel Carrier M3 as well as the 75mm Gun Motor Carriage (GMC) M3 was the 147-horsepower White 160AX gasoline engine, a six-cylinder, in-line, liquid-cooled model with a displacement of 386 cubic inches. (American Truck Historical Society)

The White 160AX engine is observed from the left side. On the side of the engine block, front to rear, are the generator, the oil-cooler assembly, and the starter. Above the oil cooler is the distributor. Above the generator is the water pump. (American Truck Historical Society)

Surprised by the savage effectiveness of German armor in the 1939-1940 Blitzkrieg, the U.S. Army Ordnance Department in June 1941 ordered an expedient self-propelled antitank gun built. It consisted of a 75mm gun M1897A4 on a Carriage M2A3 installed facing forward at the front of the crew compartment of a Half-Track Personnel Carrier M3. A pilot vehicle was quickly designed and constructed at Aberdeen Proving Ground and was designated the 75mm Gun Motor Carriage T12. When the vehicle showed promise, the Army contracted with the Autocar Co. for 86 additional examples. The pilot T12 was photographed at Aberdeen Proving ground on 21 July 1941, five days after it was first demonstrated. At this point, the vehicle lacked the armored windshield and the frames above the side doors. (Patton Museum)

With the folding armor of the door lowered, the driver is visible at the wheel of the pilot 75mm Gun Motor Carriage T12. Adjacent to the breech of the 75mm gun are a mount for a panoramic telescope and the gunner's perforated shoulder guard. (Patton Museum)

The armored windshield is in the lowered position in another 5 August 1941 photo, revealing more of the shape of the 75mm gun shield. The sighting slot on the right side of the shield would not be present on the shield of production 75mm GMC M3s. (Patton Museum)

The T12's gun shield, seen in profile in the preceding photo, is viewed from the front on 5 August 1941. The bottom-hinged armored windshield cover with sliding vision-port covers was notched at the top center to give clearance to the gun when in travel position. (Patton Museum)

A 75mm GMC T12 is viewed from the rear, showing, among other features, the door on the rear of the body and the latching mechanism to the left side of the door. On the left side of the gun shield is a storage case for the panoramic telescope. (Patton Museum)

The rear door and upper rear body panels of a T12 are removed, revealing details of the fighting compartment and 75mm gun. The gun's modified M2A3 carriage had traversing hand wheels on each side and an elevating hand wheel on the left side. (Patton Museum)

The T12's 75mm gun breech, elevation and traverse hand wheels, shoulder guard, and gun mount are viewed from the rear. The photo, dated 5 August 1941, documented the ready-ammunition storage tubes with new sprung catches. (Patton Museum)

A 21 July 1941 photograph facing the rear of the fighting compartment of a T12 shows an M25 pedestal for a machine gun at the center, fuel tanks to each side of the rear door, and hinged doors for 75mm ammunition storage bins on the floor. (Patton Museum)

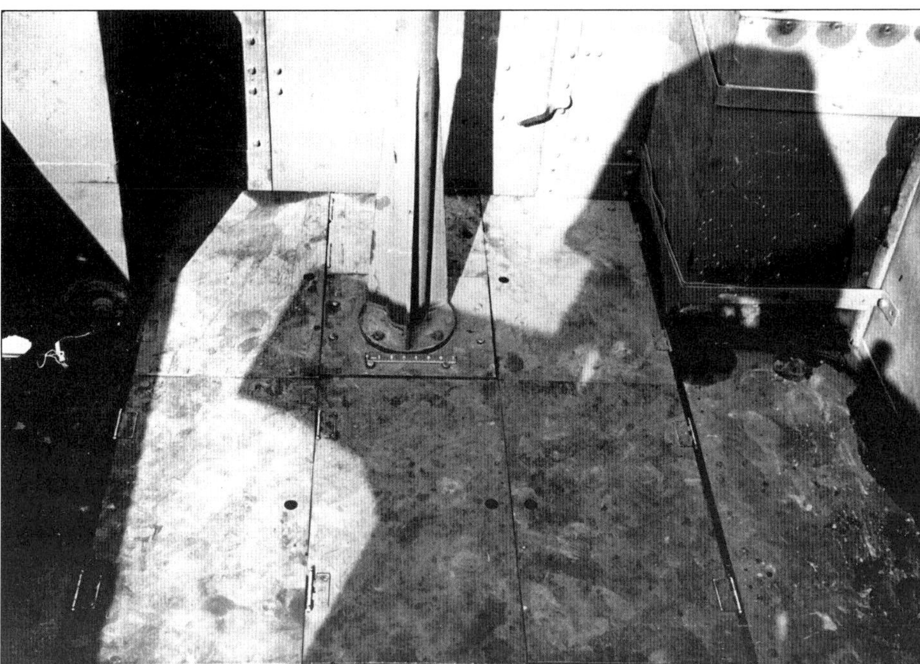

From the same vantage point as in the preceding photograph, the doors of the 75mm ammunition storage bins in the T12 are open. When closed, the doors formed the floor. The T12 could carry as many as 59 rounds of 75mm ammunition. Each round weighed between 14 and 20 pounds, depending upon type. (Patton Museum)

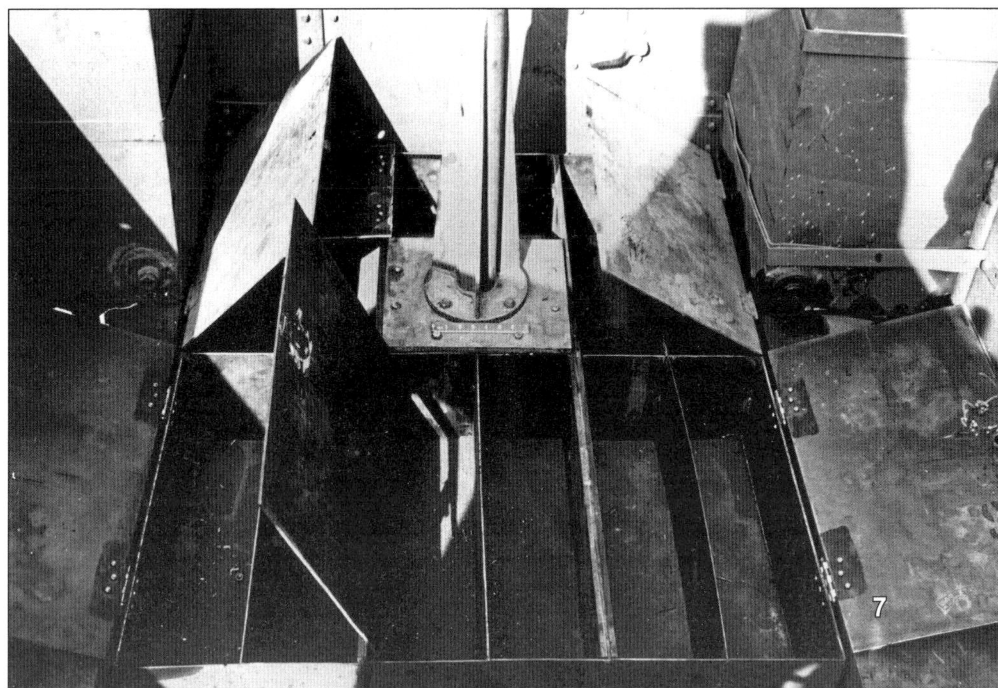

As seen on a T12 based on Half-Track Personnel Carrier M3 registration number 409527, frames above the side doors acted to support the armored windshield when raised. A Browning M2 .50-caliber machine gun is on the pedestal mount. (Patton Museum)

The machine gun mount in the T12 carried the designation Mount, Truck, Pedestal, M25. It is shown here supporting a Browning M1919A4 .30-caliber machine gun. At the bottom of the pedestal was a round flange for bolting it to the floor. (Rock Island Arsenal Museum)

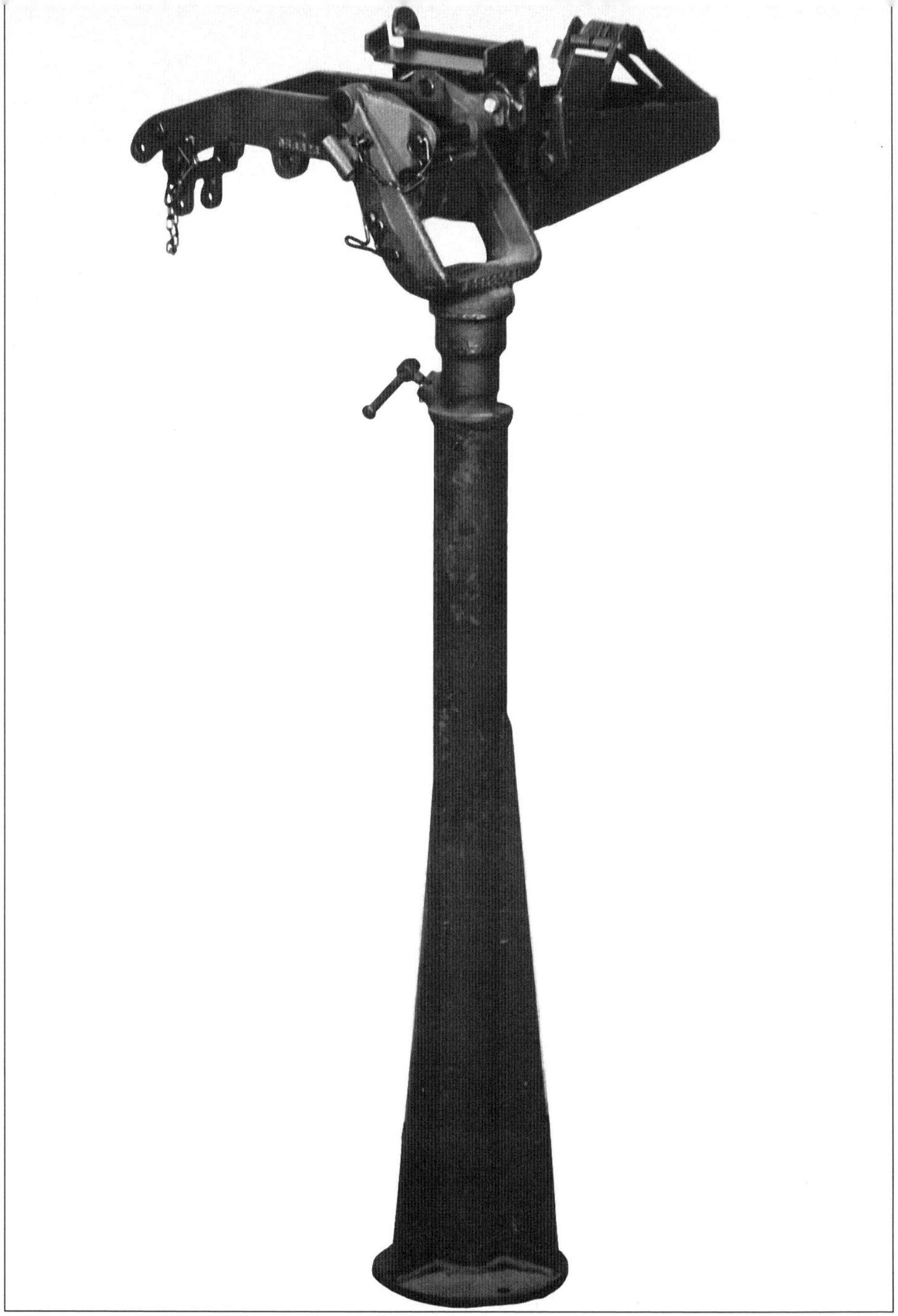

With the machine gun dismounted from the M25 pedestal mount, elements of the upper part of the mount are visible, including the cradle, which pivoted on the yoke-shaped pintle and held the gun, and the ammunition-box tray to the left of the pintle. (Rock Island Arsenal Museum)

Production examples of the T12 were tested by members of the 93rd Tank Destroyer Battalion, including this crew, manning a T12 based on White-built Half-Track Personnel Carrier M3, registration number 409545, during the Carolinas maneuvers, on 20 November 1941. (National Archives)

White-built Half-Track Personnel Carrier M3 registration number 409544, used as an interim prototype vehicle for the 75mm GMC T12 at the Aberdeen Proving Ground, exhibits a large gun shield with side wings in this 24 October 1941 photo. (Patton Museum)

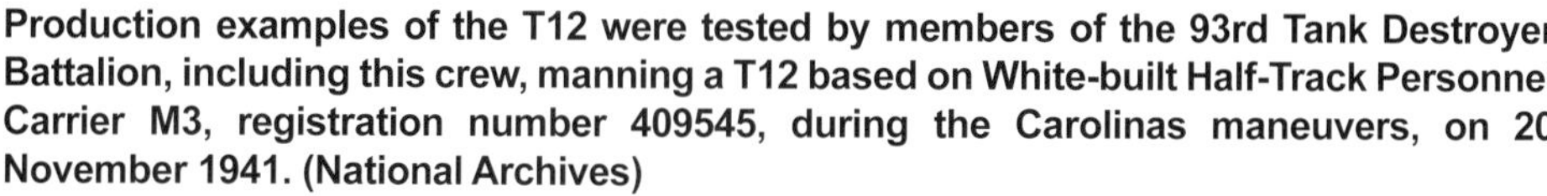

The interim prototype is viewed from the front left quarter, showing the front of the gun shield. The rods projecting from the front of the gun cradle originally served as braces for the shield of the 75mm gun on its field carriage. (TACOM LCMC History Office)

This revised gun shield with armor plates on the sides designed to give more protection to the gun crew was experimented with on a T12. Ultimately, a much trimmed-down gun shield was employed on the standardized 75mm GMC M3. (Patton Museum)

The T12 was standardized as the 75mm Gun Motor Carriage M3 on 21 November 1941. It employed an armored gun shield different from those in the preceding photos of the T12; it was attached to and moved in unison with the gun carriage. (Patton Museum)

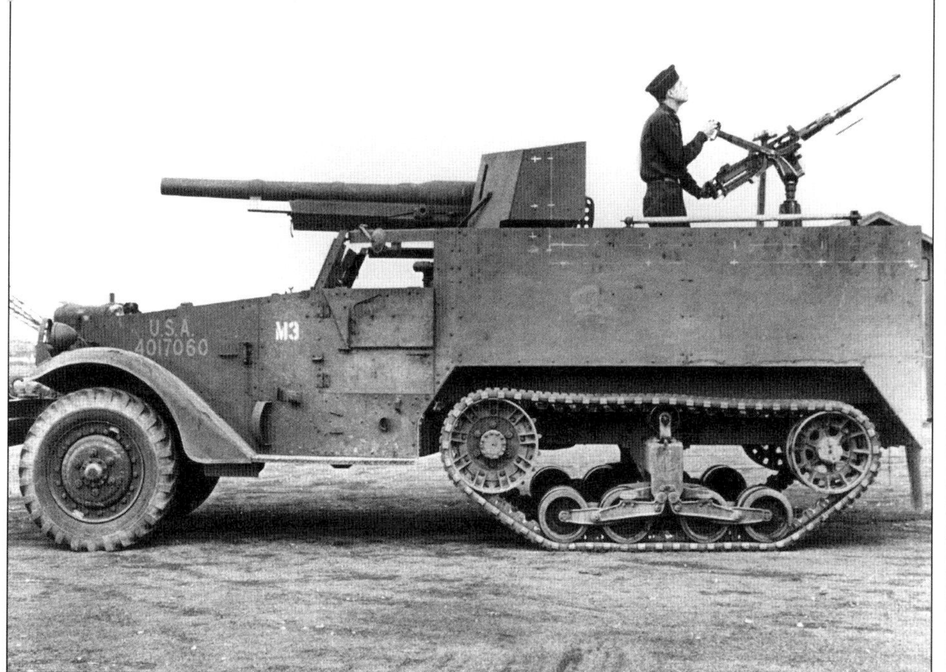

American Autocar built the 75mm Gun Motor Carriage (GMC) M3. This one, registration number 4017060, was the first to leave the factory. The gun shield had side panels to protect the gun crewmen. A soldier mans the .50-caliber machine gun. (Patton Museum)

A 75mm GMC M3 is viewed from above, showing the top panel of the gun shield. As on the 75mm GMC T12, ready-ammunition storage is below the 75mm gun mount, and a self-sealing fuel tank is situated in each rear corner of the fighting compartment. (Patton Museum)

The M3 Gun Motor Carriage as mass produced closely resembled the M3 Personnel Carrier in profile but for the gun and shield.

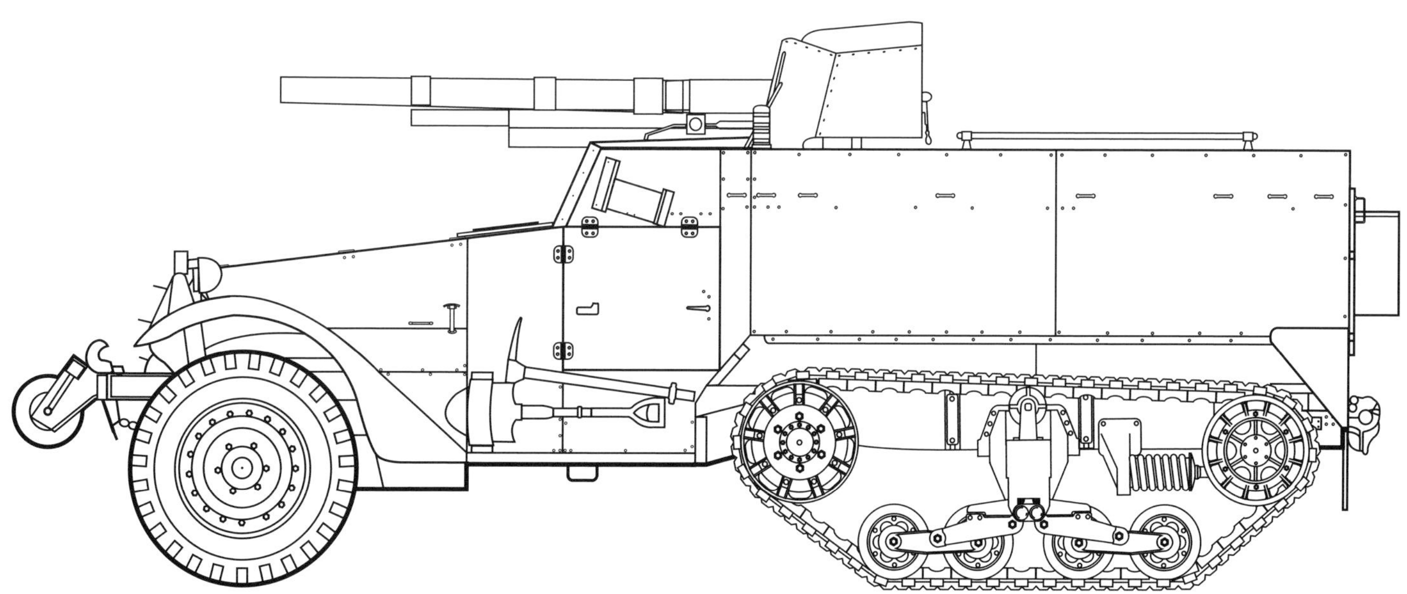

A wrecker tows a disabled 75MM GMC M3 to a maintenance facility near Shelbyville, Tennessee, during Second Army Maneuvers on 12 October 1942. A very bulky canvas cover has been arranged over the breech and the barrel of the 75mm gun. (National Archives)

A 75mm GMC M3 with an African-American crew proceeds with a column near Fort Custer, Michigan, in August 1943. In that era of a segregated U.S. military, a number of African-American tank-destroyer battalions were organized and saw combat. (National Archives)

At Camp Hood, Texas, in 1943, crews of 75mm GMC M3s stand for inspection on their vehicles. Camp Hood had been established the previous year as a training base for the Tank Destroyer Force. All vehicles feature the large, early-type headlights. (National Archives)

Crewmen of 75mm GMC M3s at Camp Hood man their vehicles sometime in 1942. The registration number of the nearest M3, 4017502, identifies it as having been produced under Contract 1765 of District 670. Two five-gallon liquid containers are on the fender. (National Archives)

Among the forces the United States Army began to position in England in 1942 were antitank battalions with the 75MM GMC M3. A Half-Track Car M2 leads a column of 75mm GMC M3s along a country lane in England on 28 October 1942. (Patton Museum)

One of the members of the crew of a 75mm GMC M3 mans the machine gun during maneuvers in England. The machine gun gave the vehicle some protection against attacks by aircraft, ground troops, and light vehicles. (Patton Museum)

The crew is alert as an M3 negotiates brushy terrain in England. This vehicle has a crew of five: the driver and the assistant driver in the cab, the gunner to the left of the breech, the loader aft of the gun, and a fifth man, probably the commander. (Patton Museum)

General Data

MODEL	M3 Gun Motor Carriage
MAKE	Autorcar
WEIGHT	20,000 pounds
LENGTH	20 feet 5½ inches
WIDTH	7 feet 1 inch
HEIGHT	8 feet 2⅝ inches
TIRE SIZES	8.25-20, 12-ply
MAX SPEED	45 mph
FUEL CAPACITY	60 gallons
RANGE	210 miles
ELECTRICAL	12 volt negative ground
TRANSMISSION SPEEDS	4
TRANSFER SPEEDS	2
TURNING RADIUS	30 feet
CREW	5

While the 75mm GMC T12 had its baptism of fire in the Philippines in late 1941, the major debut of the 75mm GMC M3 in combat was in the North Africa invasion in November 1942. This example was photographed in that theater of action. (National Archives)

On 4 March 1943 a column of 75mm GMC M3s, guns covered, pauses along a road in North Africa. Crewmen are eating canned rations. Although white star insignia apparently are on the engine hoods, other markings are conspicuously absent. (Quartermaster Museum)

A 75mm Gun Motor Carriage rests in the background as officers confer over a map in front of what is probably a M2 halftrack. This image was captured during a lull in the action at al-Qaṭṭâr ("El Guettar") in central Tunisia. (National Archives)

In 1943, 75mm GMC M3s participated in the invasion of Sicily. Around 1 August, an M3 of the Antitank Company of the 39th Infantry Regiment gingerly negotiates a very narrow lane in the village of Cerami, in the northeastern part of Sicily. (National Archives)

Three 75mm GMC M3s, operated by British Commonwealth or possibly Polish troops, are concealed underneath camouflage netting in the vicinity of Sant'Angelo near Monte Cassino, Italy. The elevation of the pieces and the static nature of the vehicles' deployment indicate they were providing indirect fire. (National Archives)

During the push through the Philippines toward the end of World War II, U.S. forces encountered one of the 75mm GMC T12s the Japanese had captured early in the war. Its distinctive gun shield is visible. Partly obscured Japanese characters on the side identify it as belonging to a unit of the Japanese occupation forces. (Patton Museum)

When stocks of 75mm guns M1897A4 were becoming depleted during 75mm GMC M3 production in early 1943, a 75mm gun M3 as used in the Sherman tank was adapted to a 75mm gun motor carriage M3, resulting in the one-off 75mm GMC T73. (Patton Museum)

As viewed from aft in a September 1943 photo, the 75mm GMC T73's main weapon was designated the 75mm gun T15, and its mount was the T17, with an M2 recoil mechanism. The T73 project was cancelled as better tank destroyers came on line. (Patton Museum)

In January 1942 the U.S. Marine Corps ordered 30 75mm GMC M3s, 30 fewer than desired because the M1897A4 guns were currently in short supply. In the fall of that year the Marines ordered 219 more M3s. The Marines referred to these vehicles in their service as the Self-Propelled Mount (SPM), but this designation apparently was not official nomenclature. Several of the USMC M3s are lined up in this photo, including USMC registration number 61656, the second to closest M3. The nearest vehicle has a holder for a 5-gallon liquid container on the cowl aft of the hood, but this feature is not present on the second vehicle. (USMC)

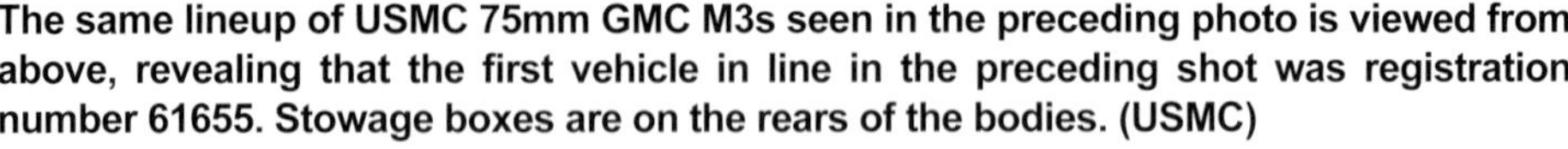
The same lineup of USMC 75mm GMC M3s seen in the preceding photo is viewed from above, revealing that the first vehicle in line in the preceding shot was registration number 61655. Stowage boxes are on the rears of the bodies. (USMC)

Sitting among stocks of chains, reinforcing rods, machinery, and vehicles being unloaded from ships at Pago Pago, American Samoa, are two 75mm GMC M3s at the center of the photo. The bulky gun cover is installed on the lead vehicle mounted to fire over the main gun shield. (National Archives)

Crewmen of a USMC 75mm GMC M3 prepare to open fire. To the left, the gunner aims the piece. At the center, the loader inserts a round into the open breech. At the right, a crewman who probably is the commander operates the breech lever. (National Archives)

The same 75mm gun in the photo at left is seen at the moment of firing during maneuvers on an island in the South Pacific in 1942. The loader is well out of the way of the recoiling breech, since normal recoil was 44.9 inches. (National Archives)

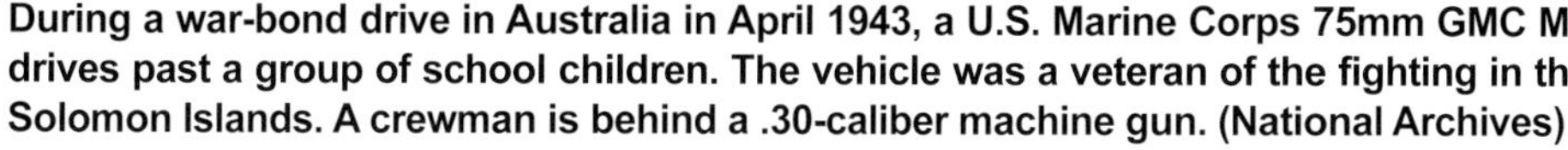

During a war-bond drive in Australia in April 1943, a U.S. Marine Corps 75mm GMC M3 drives past a group of school children. The vehicle was a veteran of the fighting in the Solomon Islands. A crewman is behind a .30-caliber machine gun. (National Archives)

Marines scrub their 75mm GMC M3 in preparation for a parade at a base in the South Pacific in July 1943. The body of the vehicle, the gun, and the gun shield were painted in an intricate yet subtle camouflage scheme mimicking jungle foliage. (National Archives)

The crews of two 75mm GMC M3s, including a few extra men on the farther vehicle, wait expectantly prior to a parade at Rowville, a suburb of Melbourne, Australia, on 29 July 1943. The nearer halftrack has a diamond-shaped marking on the door. (National Archives)

Marine vehicles, including a 75mm GMC M3 to the left, are assembled near Tetere Beach on Guadalcanal. This M3 is equipped with an unusual radio antenna mount aft of the side door: a box-shaped structure mounted at an angle. (National Archives)

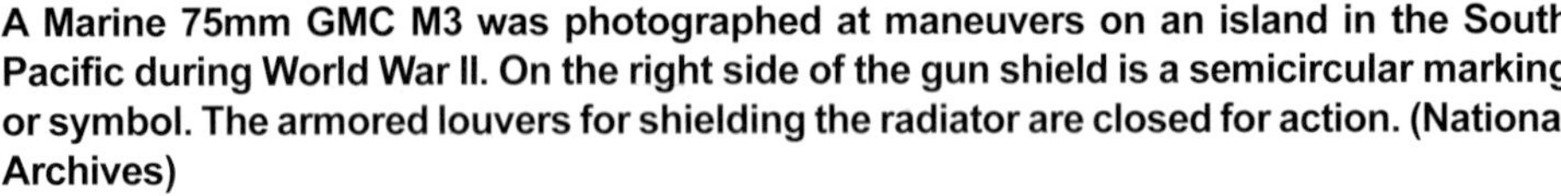

A Marine 75mm GMC M3 was photographed at maneuvers on an island in the South Pacific during World War II. On the right side of the gun shield is a semicircular marking or symbol. The armored louvers for shielding the radiator are closed for action. (National Archives)

With at least seven men aboard, a 75mm GMC M3 pauses during training maneuvers on the Mornington Peninsula in Australia in August 1943. It is not clear if the bits of brush attached to the vehicle were snagged during transit or were local camouflage. (National Archives)

In the Marine Corps, M3s often were assigned to special weapons battalions, armed with antitank and antiaircraft weapons. Here, M3 crewmen of a special weapons company undergo inspection at the 2nd Marines' base at Camp McKay, New Zealand. (National Archives)

Gunnery Sergeant James Smith and Sergeant Don Currier service the gun mount in New Guinea in October 1943. A radio antenna mount is atop the right door frame. On the cowl to the front of the driver's door is a special weapons ("SW") unit symbol. (National Archives)

Marine 75mm GMC M3s with an abundance of .30-caliber and .50-caliber machine guns conduct training on a beach in November 1943. Curiously, the chassis and bodies are Half-Track Car M2, not the typical Half-Track Personnel Carrier M3. (National Archives)

Two U.S. Marine Corps 75mm GMC M3s are parked at a base in New Guinea. "USMC" is stenciled on the side of the hood of the closer vehicle, and a pedestal mount with pintle and cradle but with machine gun dismounted is in the fighting compartment. (National Archives)

A Marine 75mm GMC M3 is poised for action on Cape Gloucester on the island of New Britain in late 1943 or early 1944. A close view of the photo reveals that tire chains are present as an aid to traction. A crewman mans a .30-caliber machine gun. (National Archives)

On a landing beach at Cape Gloucester, New Britain, in late December 1943, LST-202 disgorges a USMC 75mm GMC M3. The vehicle was painted overall in Olive Drab, while some M3s landing there had multi-color camouflage. (USMC)

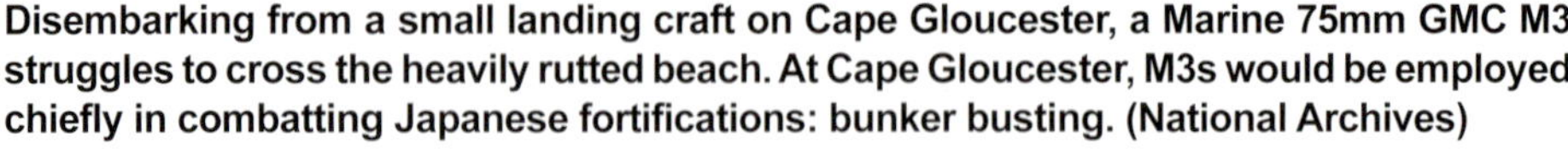

Disembarking from a small landing craft on Cape Gloucester, a Marine 75mm GMC M3 struggles to cross the heavily rutted beach. At Cape Gloucester, M3s would be employed chiefly in combatting Japanese fortifications: bunker busting. (National Archives)

Modified to approximate M3 standards, a camouflaged Marine M2 exits an LST at Cape Gloucester on 26 December 1943. A .30-caliber machine gun is over the assistant driver's seat and at least two .50-cal. machine guns are in the fighting compartment. (USMC)

An M3 coming ashore at Cape Gloucester displays interesting details. The early-type headlights have been removed but their brush guards remain. A pintle mount for a machine gun is on the hood, and wire has been strung for applying foliage. (National Archives)

Main Gun Data

Model	75mm Gun M1897A4
Total Weight	1,026 pounds
Type of Breechlock	Nordenfeld
Rifling	24 grooves, uniform right-hand twist, 7° slope
Length of Rifling	87.37 inches
Overall Length	107.13 inches
Primer	Percussion
Maximum Rate of Fire	6 rounds per minute
Maximum Powder Pressure	38,000 p.s.i.
Muzzle Velocity, firing Armor Piercing	2,000 ft/sec
Muzzle Velocity, firing High Explosive	1,950 ft/sec
Muzzle Energy APC	415 ft-tons (long tons)
Muzzle Energy AP/HE	387 ft-tons (long tons)
Maximum Range, APC/HE	13,870 yards, independent of mount
Maximum Range, AP	10,520 yards, independent of mount

In a photo dated 26 February 1944, a 75mm GMC M3 stands ready for further action, with several dead Japanese in the left foreground. A curved camouflage pattern is visible on the driver's door. At the rear is a .30-caliber machine gun. (National Archives)

A close inspection of the .50-caliber ammunition box on a 75mm GMC M3 on a Pacific island, possibly Namur, reveals a Unit Numerical Identification System (UNIS) code, 402 inside a semicircle, symbolizing Weapons Company, 4th Marine Regiment, 4th Marine Division. (National Archives)

U.S. Marines, one of them with the 402-and-semicircle UNIS code on his jacket and ammunition box, advance during the invasion of Namur Island in the Marshall Islands in early 1944. In the left background, the rear of a 75MM GMC M3 is visible. (National Archives)

On 2 February 1944 a radio-equipped 75mm GMC M3 picks its way through rubble on Namur. The small, light-colored shape on the side of the body below the 75mm gun shield was a Vargas girl, one of the popular pinups by artist Alberto Vargas. (USMC)

A USMC 75mm GMC M3 fires at Japanese targets on Saipan in the Mariana Islands in June 1944. Two Browning .30-caliber machine guns are visible in the fighting compartment, and a radio antenna mount is on top of the right door frame of the cab. (National Archives)

As the Marines begin to sweep from the hills of Saipan toward the coast and ultimate victory, a camouflage-painted M3 engages targets above the coastal town of Garapan. Numerous knapsacks are hanging from the side of the half-track's body. (USMC)

Marine infantrymen crowd around a 75mm GMC M3 positioned on a hill overlooking Japanese positions at Makunsha, Saipan. A close view is offered of the radio antenna mount on the door frame. The letter A is painted on the gun shield. (National Archives)

Crewmen of an M3 take a quick break alongside a wrecked building, reportedly in Saipan. Packs, bayonets, and entrenching tools are stowed on the rear of the body. A folded tarpaulin is on the fender. To the lower right of the rear of the body is a metal bucket. A .30-caliber machine gun is mounted in the left rear corner of the vehicle. (USMC)

On 25 June 1944 a U.S. Marine Corps 75mm GMC M3 blasts away at Japanese forces on the road to Chacha, Saipan. The driver's door is open and his leg is sticking out of it. To the left, a Marine observes the effect of the 75mm gun's fire through binoculars. The crew apparently had been interrupted from performing repairs on the front tire, as a lug wrench is still attached to one of the lug bolts. Driving through the wreckage of houses and buildings posed definite hazards to tires. (USMC)

A 75mm GMC M3 with the gun crew hunkered down in the fighting compartment accompanies Marines proceeding down a road in Saipan. The vehicle exhibits a subtle three-color camouflage scheme. The machine guns are fitted with canvas covers. (USMC)

Below some of the bluffs that are a prominent feature of Saipan's topography, a Marine M3 stands by to support an infantry operation. Secured to the side of the body of the vehicle are the two wooden poles that screwed together to form the bore-brush staff. (USMC)

An amtrac passes a Marine 75mm GMC M3 parked along a dusty road in Saipan. The right side of the hood has been opened, probably to cool the engine. The tires exhibit different tread patterns. This M3 is equipped with a roller at the front of the chassis, and a tow cable is wound around the roller. The early-style headlights have been removed. These units were susceptible to blast damage from the 75mm gun. Later in M3 production, easily removable headlights were introduced to these vehicles. (USMC)

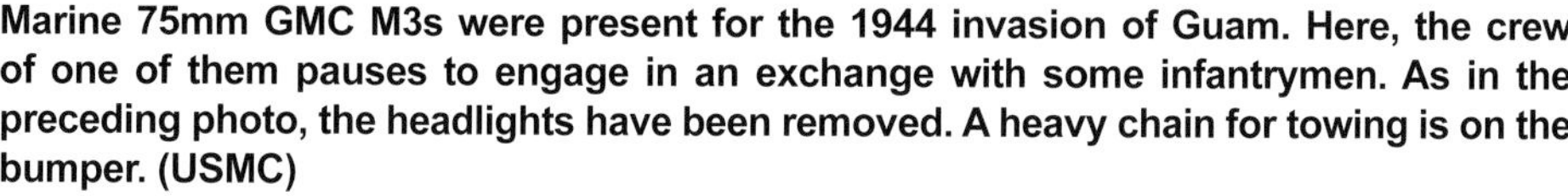

Marine 75mm GMC M3s were present for the 1944 invasion of Guam. Here, the crew of one of them pauses to engage in an exchange with some infantrymen. As in the preceding photo, the headlights have been removed. A heavy chain for towing is on the bumper. (USMC)

A Marine M3 painted in three-color camouflage fires on a Japanese machine gun position. Although the original caption did not list the location, it apparently was taken on Saipan. A rifle or carbine holster has been attached to the front of the driver's door. (USMC)

Chains are visible on the moving tires of this USMC M3 as it rolls past a column of infantry. The camouflage scheme includes dark-colored borders between the colors. On the fender is the 1st Marine Division's diamond-shaped UNIS. (U.S. Army Engineer History Office)

The 75mm gun of this Marine M3 has just been fired at a target across a body of water, and the barrel is in full recoil. In the foreground, an observer watches through binoculars to determine the accuracy of the fire and issue corrections to the gunner if necessary. (USMC)

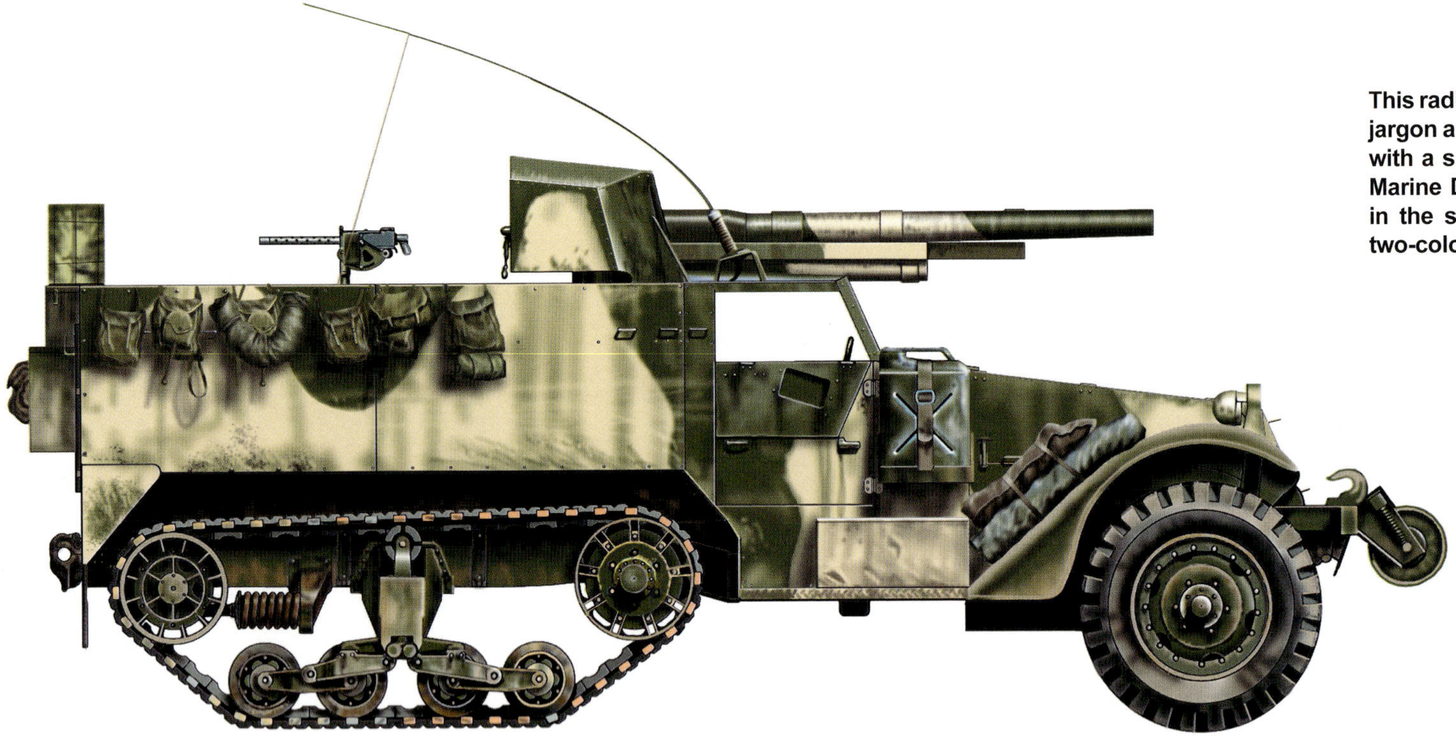

This radio-equipped 75mm GMC M3 (in USMC jargon a self-propelled mount or SPM) served with a special weapons company in the 2nd Marine Division during the Tinian Campaign in the summer of 1944. It featured a wavy, two-color camouflage scheme.

A Marine M3 fires on Japanese positions on Tinian on 30 July 1944. The large pile of pasteboard 75mm ammunition packing tubes attests to the volume of fire the gun has unleashed. Much stowed equipment is present on the vehicle, including a drum, possibly for fuel, oil, or water. (National Archives)

In a photograph reportedly taken on Tinian, a 75mm GMC M3 lies disabled along a road, possibly a victim of a land mine. The right track has been severed and the right front wheel and tire are missing. It is not clear if this vehicle was salvageable. (National Archives)

A 75mm GMC M3 moves into a canebrake on Tinian on 30 July 1944, clearing a way for infantry. In addition to the two storage boxes mounted on the rear of the vehicle, an interesting array of stowed gear is present – including a drum for fuel, oil, or water – with a petcock wired under the right storage box, a box wired under the left storage box, a spare tire mounted on the rear door, and entrenching shovels and ammunition tubes at the bottom. (National Archives)

Marine infantrymen, including one with a radio pack, advance behind a 75mm GMC M3 on Peleliu in September 1944. Stored in a rack on the upper left corner of the rear of the body are two .50-caliber Ammunition Chests M2 with a capacity of 200 rounds each. (National Archives)

During a brief break in the action during the September 1944 battle for the island of Peleliu, Marines gather around a well-weathered 75mm GMC M3. A .50-caliber machine gun and a .30-caliber machine gun are mounted in the fighting compartment. (National Archives)

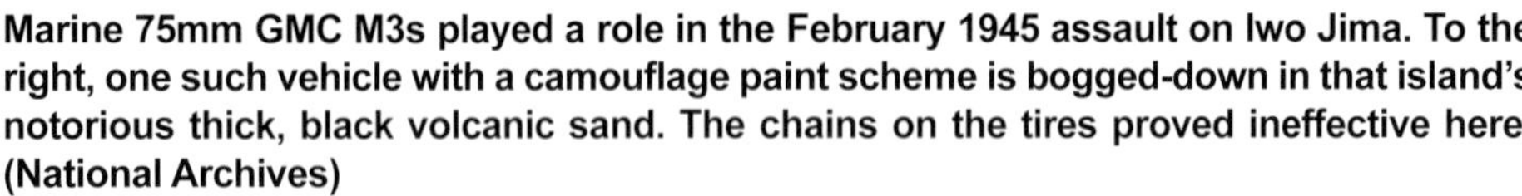

Marine 75mm GMC M3s played a role in the February 1945 assault on Iwo Jima. To the right, one such vehicle with a camouflage paint scheme is bogged-down in that island's notorious thick, black volcanic sand. The chains on the tires proved ineffective here. (National Archives)

During the battle for Iwo Jima, the Marines used their M3s, including *Tarheel,* photographed on 25 February 1945. A large dent is on the roller, the left fender is crumpled, and sandbags are on the hood. A chain is on the right tire. (National Archives)

A 75mm GMC M3 of the 9th Marine Regiment blasts at Japanese entrenchments on cliffs. Although the location of this photograph was not specified, the 9th Marines fought in the Bougainville, Guam, and Iwo Jima campaigns during World War II. (National Archives)

Tarheel and her crew pause for a photo at Camp Pendleton, California, before departing for combat. The restoration on the following pages was based on this vehicle, and standing in the cab is Sgt. Hank Backlund, who assisted with the restoration. (Hank Backlund collection)

Tarheel, the USMC 75mm GMC M3 that saw combat on Iwo Jima and that is the subject of the two preceding photographs, has been memorialized in a rare surviving M3. This 75mm GMC M3, Ordnance Department serial number, M3-75-1939, was purchased by a Hollywood studio after World War II. Shorn of its 75mm gun mount, it was featured as a German half-track in the 1960s television series *Rat Patrol.* In recent years, Brent Mullins Jeep Parts restored the vehicle to resemble Hank Backlund's *Tarheel.* (David Doyle)

Tires specified for the M3 were 12-ply 8.25-20 combat tires. This wheel is the late type without the six large openings. The wheel was mounted with six lug nuts. The fender was stamped steel with pronounced contours and a raised rim around it for strengthening. (David E. Harper)

Under the left headlight assembly is a channel-shaped fender support. Running up the channel of the support and secured in place with three small holders is a power cable for the headlight and blackout marker lamp. To the left are the bumper, tow hook, and roller. (David E. Harper)

Viewing under the left fender, the fender support is to the left, and a flange on the inboard side of the fender is bolted to the armored body above the support. On the frame is stamped this vehicle's manufacturer's serial number, M3-75-1939. A flexible rubber brake line protrudes through the frame. (David E. Harper)

The service headlight, the small, separate blackout marker lamp on the left fender, and the brush guard are the early types used on the 75mm GMC M3. Later in production, a smaller, easily removable headlight with attached blackout marker was employed. (David E. Harper)

The power cable for the headlight comes up through a grommeted hole in the fender and into the rear of the headlight case. Although the early headlights were not easily detachable, they sometimes were removed to preserve them from blast damage. (David E. Harper)

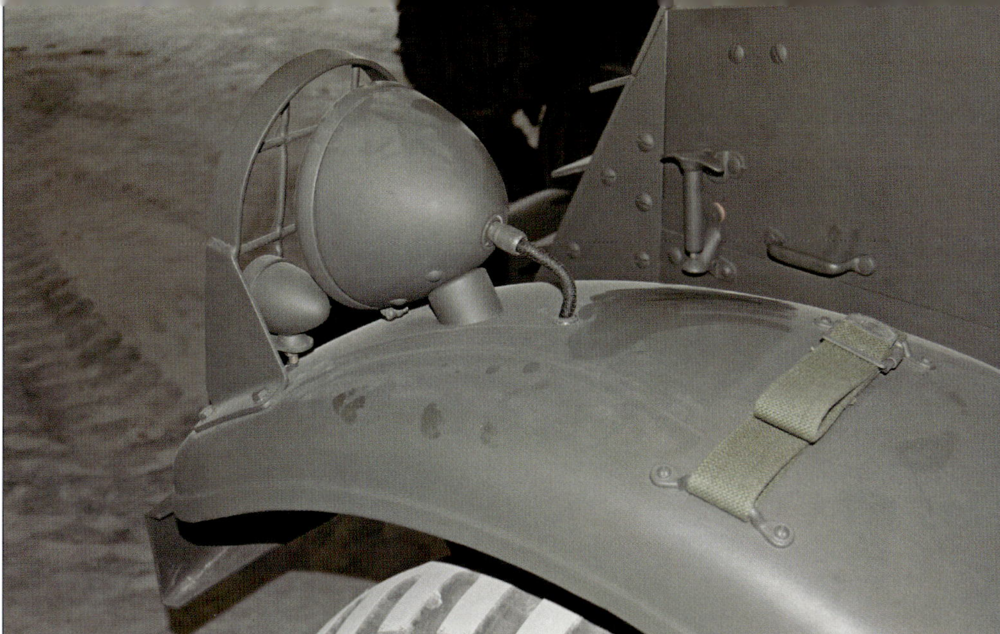

The cylindrical, tilted support of the left headlight assembly is shown. Aft of the left headlight assembly are two footman loops with a webbing strap attached for securing a folded tarpaulin on the fender. On the side of the hood are a hood clamp and a handle. (David E. Harper)

The front end is viewed from the left side. The four armored slats on the front of the body were hinged and were opened to ventilate the radiator. During combat, they were closed to prevent damage to the radiator. Some of the front left suspension is in view. (David Doyle)

With the left side of the hood of *Tarheel* open, part of the engine, right, and the radiator fan and the radiator, center, are visible. The black object at the bottom is the Delco-Remy generator. Above the generator and to the rear of the belts is the water pump. (David E. Harper)

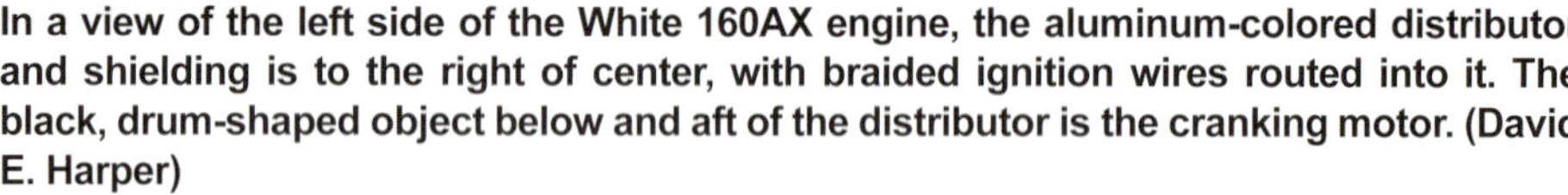

In a view of the left side of the White 160AX engine, the aluminum-colored distributor and shielding is to the right of center, with braided ignition wires routed into it. The black, drum-shaped object below and aft of the distributor is the cranking motor. (David E. Harper)

On the forward (left in the photo) side of the aluminum-colored shielding for the distributor is a piano hinge, for opening and removing the shielding. To the right, the black box with the red manufacturer's data plate is the Delco-Remy voltage regulator. (David E. Harper)

On top of the cylinder head, inboard of the distributor, is the thermostat housing. The large, flexible hose provided ventilation air to the cab. Stamped on the engine block to the lower right is "160AX / 5326," representing the engine model and serial number. (David E. Harper)

Toward the left rear of the engine compartment of *Tarheel* is a surge tank that is original to this vehicle. The tank has a red and white placard identifying it as made by the Young radiator company and cautioning not to remove the cap when the engine is hot. (David E. Harper)

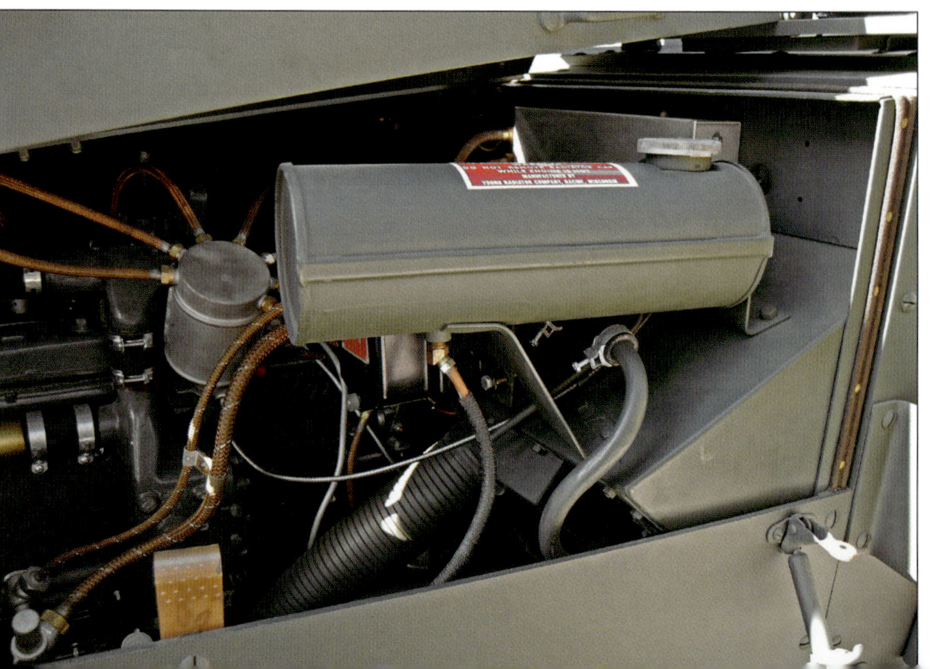

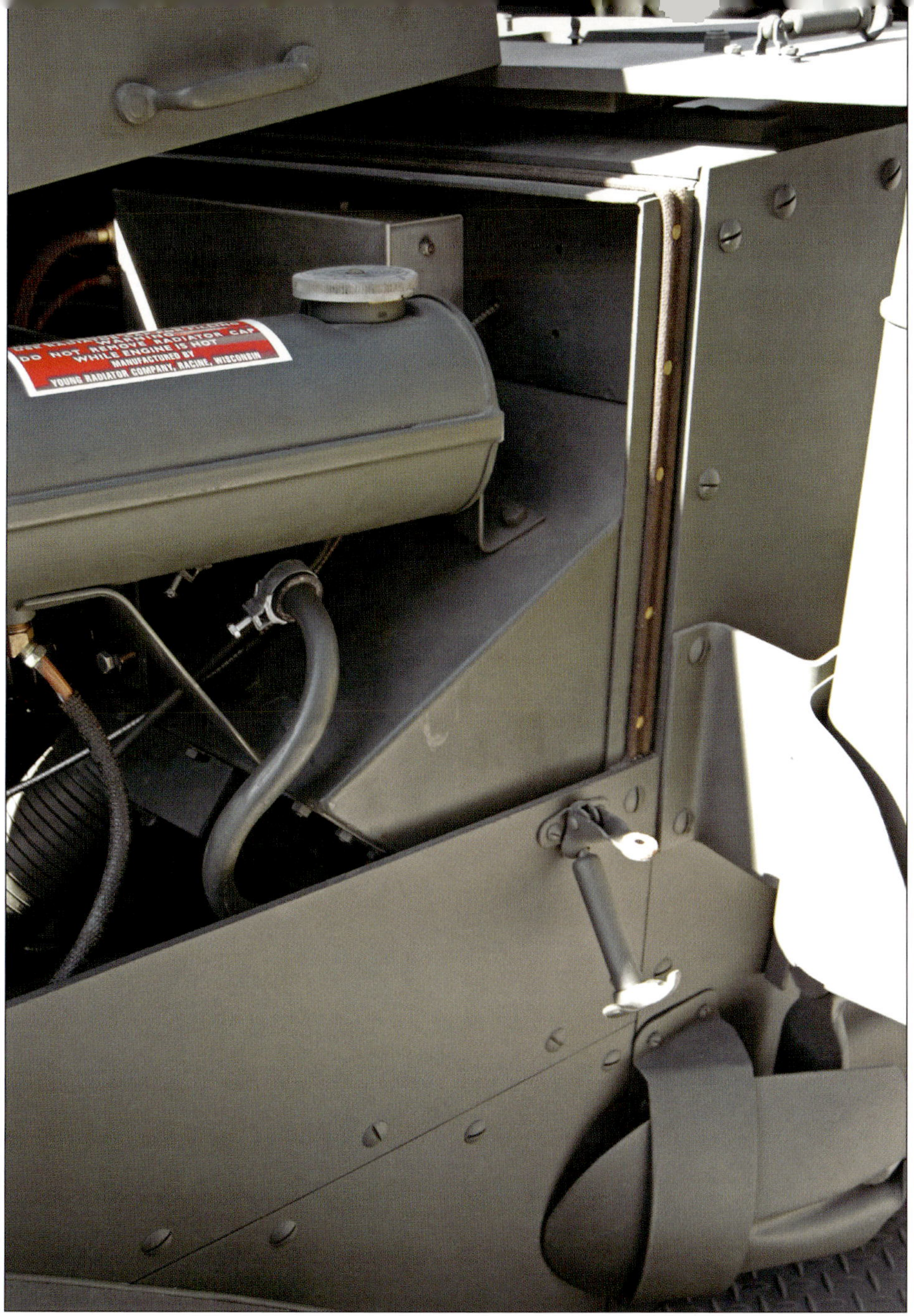

The left rear corner of the engine compartment is viewed with the hood open. At the top is the grab handle on the rear of the hood. Attached to the rim around the opening of the engine compartment is a gasket to provide a weather seal when the hood is secured shut. Fastened to the armor of the body below the opening of the engine compartment is a hold-down clamp for the hood. (David E. Harper)

The forward left part of the engine compartment is displayed with the hood open. Fastened to the side of the hood are a grab handle and a catch for the hold-down clamp. The associated hold-down clamp is at the bottom of the engine compartment opening, lying down on the fender. The rolled, face-hardened steel body armor here had a specified thickness of ¼ inch. (David E. Harper)

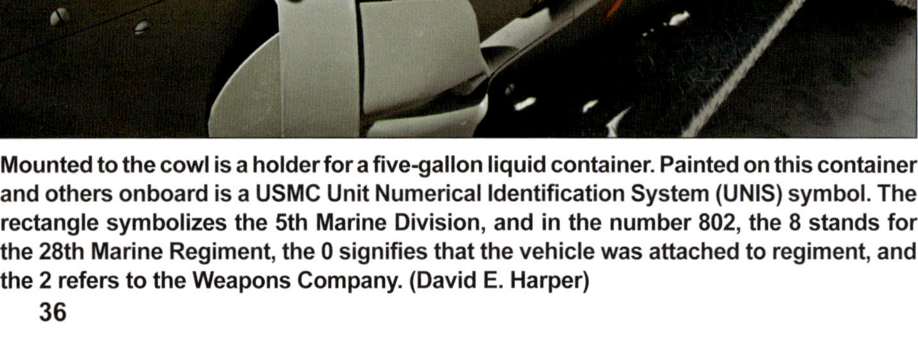

Mounted to the cowl is a holder for a five-gallon liquid container. Painted on this container and others onboard is a USMC Unit Numerical Identification System (UNIS) symbol. The rectangle symbolizes the 5th Marine Division, and in the number 802, the 8 stands for the 28th Marine Regiment, the 0 signifies that the vehicle was attached to regiment, and the 2 refers to the Weapons Company. (David E. Harper)

The rear of the five-gallon liquid container holder is displayed. The rear of the holder is secured with one slotted, oval-headed screw toward the bottom and with a door stop that is fastened over the middle of the holder with two slotted, oval-headed screws. Also in view are the hinges of the driver's door and, to the far right, the bolt assembly for locking the top panel of the door when lowered. (David E. Harper)

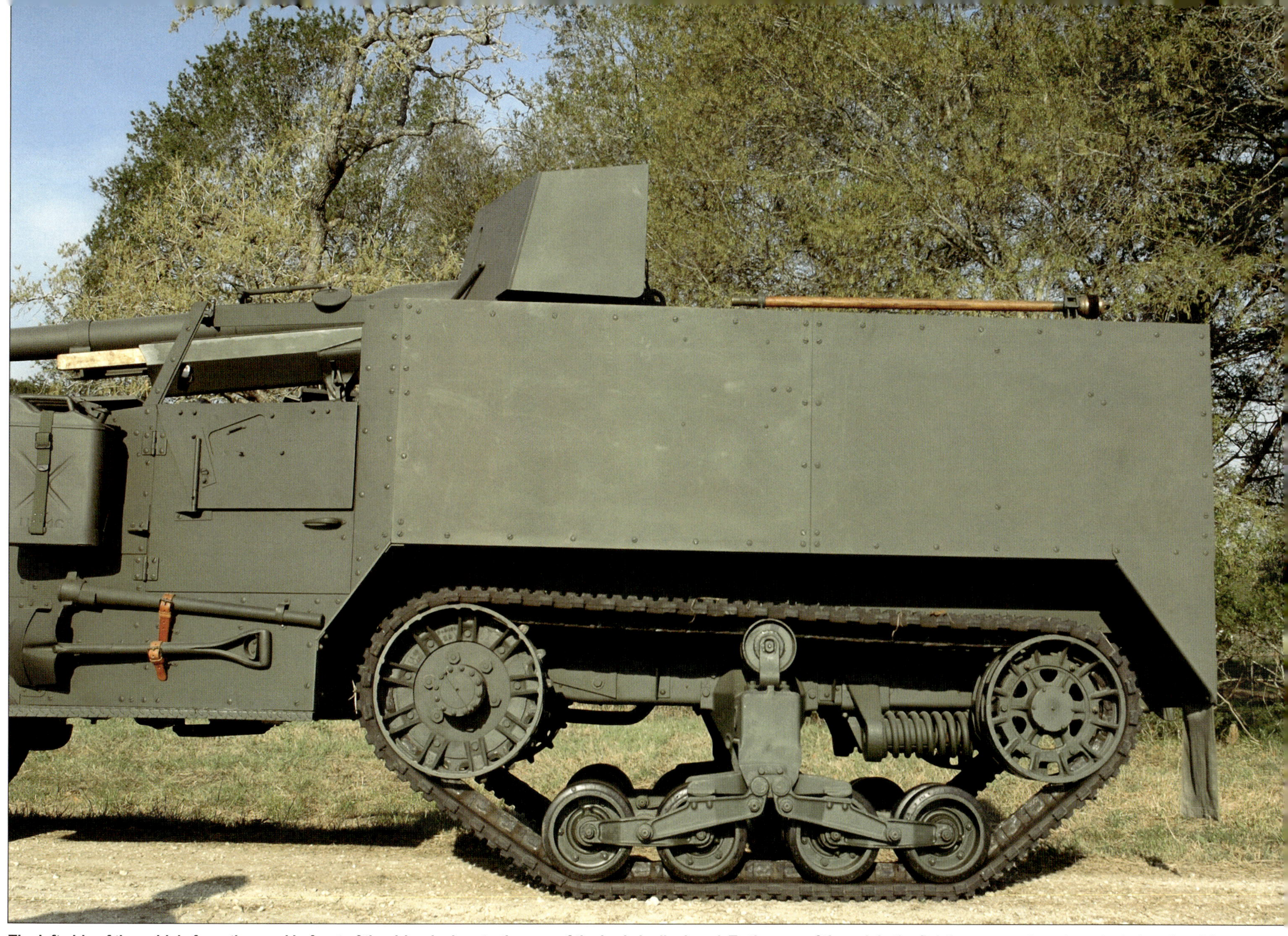

The left side of the vehicle from the cowl in front of the driver's door to the rear of the body is displayed. To the rear of the cab is the fighting compartment, protected on the sides and rear by ¼-inch rolled, face-hardened steel armor, but offering no overhead protection. Above the top of the fighting compartment is the left side of the shield of the 75mm gun M1897A4. The overall design of the tracked suspension is exhibited. (David Doyle)

Stored on the side of the vehicle below the driver's door are a mattock and handle and a shovel. They rest on brackets and are secured in place with leather straps. To the lower left are footman loops and a webbing strap for securing a folded tarpaulin to the fender. (David E. Harper)

The track suspension of the 75mm GMC M3 consists of an endless rubber and steel track that revolves around a drive sprocket to the front, an idler wheel at the rear, and a bogie assembly at the center with four rollers at the bottom and a track-support roller at the top. (David Doyle)

Details of the rear part of the left running board, with a diamond-tread pattern on it, and the exterior door-operating handle are shown. Between the rear of the cab and the front of the track is a mud guard that tapers to the top. The grip of the shovel handle fits over a D-shaped bracket attached to the body. To the upper left is the upper panel of the door, folded down. (David E. Harper)

The left drive sprocket is viewed close-up. The teeth in the middle of the drive-sprocket assembly engaged the track guides at the center of the inner side of the track to propel the track. Also in view are the bogie rollers. These are fitted with 12-4 1/8 rubber tires. (David E. Harper)

The drive sprocket assembly consists of an inner and an outer flange with a drive sprocket sandwiched between them. Spokes and lightening holes were designed into the flanges, giving them more of a framework type of appearance than one of solidity. (David E. Harper)

A heavy steel casting formed the basis for the left bogie assembly, with a similar casting used on the right. Bolting steel crossbars to two continuous steel cables and molding rubber around those assemblies formed the tracks. Steel track guides were fastened to the centers of the crossbars. (David E. Harper)

Fastened to the top of the left bogie bracket is the mount for the track-support roller. The tapering objects visible within the bogie bracket are the two vertical volute springs that buffer the suspension. Several casting marks are present on the bogie bracket. (David E. Harper)

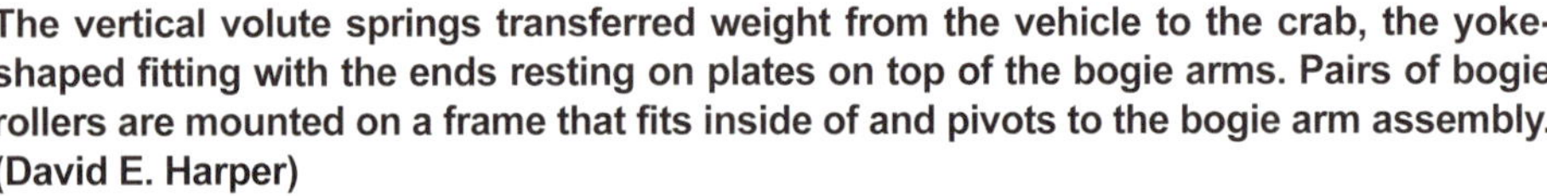

The vertical volute springs transferred weight from the vehicle to the crab, the yoke-shaped fitting with the ends resting on plates on top of the bogie arms. Pairs of bogie rollers are mounted on a frame that fits inside of and pivots to the bogie arm assembly. (David E. Harper)

The idler wheel assemblies consist of inner and outer flanges with a rather light-duty appearance, replete with many lightening holes, with a space in the center to give clearance to the track guides. These wheels are adjustable for fine-tuning track tension. (David E. Harper)

In front of each idler wheel is a dual coil spring. As originally designed, these chassis had rigid idler mounts, making them prone to throwing tracks when negotiating rough ground. The addition of the springs allowed the idlers to flex, solving the problem. (David E. Harper)

The rear of the left track is viewed above the idler wheel. Small rubber sprues are visible on the corners of the track treads. At the center is a guard for the rear of the taillight assembly. A triangular gusset is attached to the side armor and the rear panel of the body. (David E. Harper)

On top of the left side of the body is stored a section of the bore-brush staff for the 75mm gun. It is secured in place with two clamps welded to the sill. The brush end of the staff is in view. (David E. Harper)

Cast rings retained the handle end of the bore brush when stowed atop the vehicle side. Another section of the staff was stored on the opposite side of the body. (David Harper)

After the bulk of the outdoors photos of *Tarheel* were taken, two stowage boxes and a holder for a bucket were added to the rear of the body to complete the vehicle. Below the left box are the left tail-light assembly and an electrical receptacle with a flip cover for a towed trailer. (David Doyle)

A close-up look at the lower left part of the right stowage box on *Tarheel* shows how these boxes are attached to the rear of the body with slotted oval-headed screws through flanges protruding from the boxes. Also in view is the center hinge of the rear door. (David Doyle)

The rear of *Tarheel* is displayed before the stowage boxes and the bucket holder were installed. To the left of the rear door is the door's locking mechanism. Below the door is the tow pintle. At the bottom of the body of the vehicle on each side of the tow pintle are bumperettes, shaped like shallow channel sections and protruding only very slightly from the body. Above the top of the body, the upper rear of the 75mm gun shield is visible. (David E. Harper)

Tarheel is observed from the left rear quarter, showing the positioning of the bore-brush staff at the top of the body. The side of the body alongside the fighting compartment comprised two plates of ¼-inch rolled, face-hardened steel armor. (David Doyle)

The tow pintle, viewed from the right side, consists of a hook with a latch on top, mounted so as to rotate on its longitudinal axis. On the forward end of the pintle sleeve, hidden from view, is a coil spring to protect the chassis from the shock of sudden starts. (David E. Harper)

Looking underneath the rear of the frame of *Tarheel,* the tow pintle bracket is visible, with the hook of the tow pintle at the top center. A portion of the coil spring of the tow pintle is visible forward of the hook. To the lower right is the right idler wheel assembly. (David E. Harper)

Toward the top left, above the left idler stop screw, is the left idler-post brace, with an adjusting nut in the center. To the rear of the axle toward the bottom of the photograph is a horizontal tube that serves to connect and reinforce the left and right bogie frames. (David E. Harper)

In another view under the frame, to the top right and top left are the idler stop screws, which are adjustable and act to limit the rearward swing of the idler-wheel shackles and the idler wheels. Linked to the front of each shackle is an idler spring assembly. (David E. Harper)

A view is provided of the inner side of the right idler-wheel assembly and related parts, including the idler stop screw and bracket, shackle, and idler spring. Also in view is the inner side of the right bogie assembly, including the vertical volute springs. (David E. Harper)

The left rear suspension is viewed from underneath the rear of *Tarheel.* A clear view is offered of the manner in which the shaft at the rear of the idler spring is attached to the bottom front of the idler shackle. The spring consists of an inner and an outer coil spring. (David E. Harper)

There are four bogie rollers per side of the 75mm GMC M3. They are mounted in tandem, two to the front and two to the rear of the bogie bracket. The pairs are mounted in frame assemblies, which in turn ride on pivoting bearings on the bogie arms. (David E. Harper)

The rear axle and differential are viewed from the rear. To each side of the axle is a brake drum and a drive sprocket. The sprocket teeth are visible at the center of the drive sprocket assembly to the left. Routed above the right side of the rear axle is the exhaust. (David E. Harper)

Partially visible to the front of the rear axle in the background are the gray-colored transfer case, which is connected directly to the rear of the transmission. To the rear of the front axle is a green skid plate, which protects the bottom of the engine-oil pan. (David E. Harper)

The 75mm ammunition boxes in the fighting compartment of this M3 GMC have been removed, exposing the chassis frame. In the center foreground is the coil spring and bracket for the tow pintle, and the 75mm ammunition ready rack is in the background. (David Doyle)

Although devoid of the 75mm gun mount, the steel structure that provided a base for the gun mount and a housing for the 75mm ready-ammunition rack is intact in this vehicle. In the background are the cab and windshield cover. (David Doyle)

The rear door-locking mechanism is attached to the body of the vehicle to the left of the rear door. It consists of an operating handle linked to an upper and a lower latch rod, each of which is secured in two guides. To lock the door, the end of each rod engages a latch bracket fastened to the left side of the door. A coil spring is around the upper part of the upper rod. Also in view are the electrical receptacle for a trailer and the left tail-light assembly. (David E. Harper)

The rear door of *Tarheel* is swung open, showing the folding seat on the inner side of the door. It consists of a folding seat bottom and a fixed seat back, both of which are fitted with cushions with water-resistant covers. Visible inside the fighting compartment are the 75mm gun and mount and, on the floor, the 75mm ammunition boxes. Two more crew seats are located on the sides of the fighting compartment. (David Doyle)

The folding seat on the rear door is shown from a closer perspective. When the seat bottom was folded down for use, it rested on the floor created by the doors on top of the 75mm ammunition boxes. Welded to the top or forward end of the seat bottom is a channel section. Projecting from the left edge of the rear door are the upper and the lower latch brackets. These brackets are fastened to the door with slotted oval-headed screws and hex nuts. (David E. Harper)

As seen through the open rear door, the 75mm ammunition boxes extend to the rear of the fighting compartment and are raised considerably higher than the original floor of the Half-Track Personnel Carrier M3, which was even with the bottom of the door. (David Doyle)

Sixty-gallon, rubber-covered fuel tanks are secured with brackets in the rear corners of the fighting compartment. To the side of the folded seat on the rear door is the interior operating handle of the door-locking mechanism. A sill is attached to the top of the body. (David E. Harper)

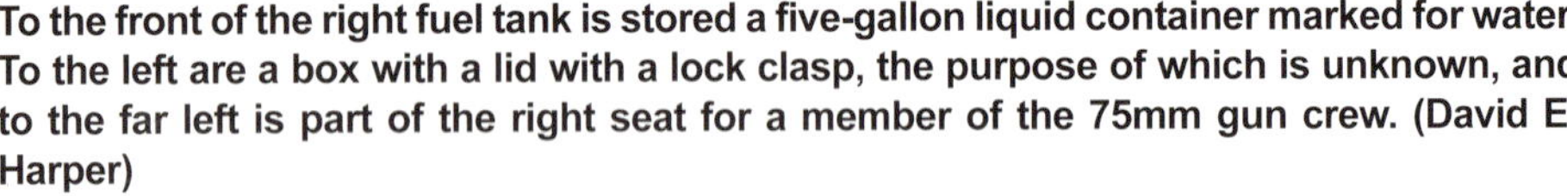

To the front of the right fuel tank is stored a five-gallon liquid container marked for water. To the left are a box with a lid with a lock clasp, the purpose of which is unknown, and to the far left is part of the right seat for a member of the 75mm gun crew. (David E. Harper)

The right fuel tank and the five-gallon liquid container are viewed from above. The fuel tanks were of bullet-sealing design. On top of the tank are the filler cap and the top of the electrically operated fuel gauge, which consists of a float assembly and a rheostat. (David E. Harper)

The sill around the interior top of the fighting compartment is viewed at the right rear corner of the compartment. A triangular gusset is welded to the corner of the sill. Mounted in a clamp on top of the sill is a section of the 75mm bore-brush staff. (David E. Harper)

The left rear corner of the fighting compartment is observed, with the left fuel tank at the center. The steel floor plates in this area also served as lids for compartments below that contain up to 40 rounds of 75mm ammunition as well as vehicular equipment. (David E. Harper)

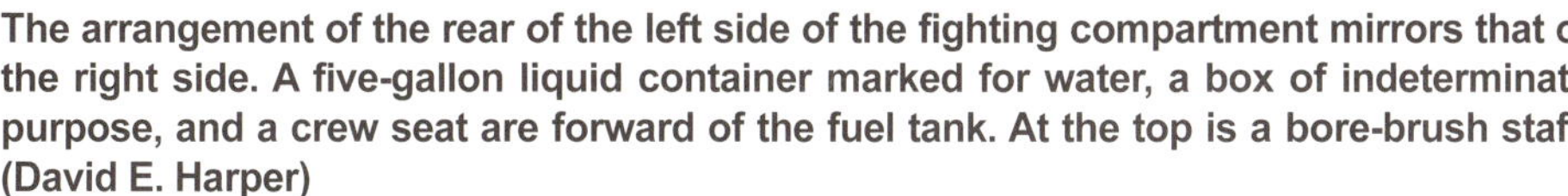
The arrangement of the rear of the left side of the fighting compartment mirrors that of the right side. A five-gallon liquid container marked for water, a box of indeterminate purpose, and a crew seat are forward of the fuel tank. At the top is a bore-brush staff. (David E. Harper)

The hinged lids of the ammunition and equipment bins in the rear of the fighting compartment are viewed from the right side of the breech of the 75mm gun. Four of the lids have wire handles, while the two small lids have holes in them for pulling them open. (David E. Harper)

The left fuel tank of *Tarheel* is viewed from above. The green-colored filler cap has a C-shaped wire handle to assist in unscrewing it. The aluminum-colored top and electrical wires of the fuel gauge are outboard of the filler cap. Atop the sill is a bore-brush staff. (David E. Harper)

The folding rear seat, interior of the rear door, the hinged lids on the floor, and the left fuel tank are displayed. The screws and nuts to the sides of the rear door are for fastening the door hinges and locking mechanism as well as vertical steel reinforcing strips. (David E. Harper)

The 75mm Gun M1897A4 and its mount and shield are viewed from the rear. The gun mount was the 75mm Gun Mount M3, which essentially was formed from the components above the suspension and the trails of the Gun Carriage M2A3, which was a towed mount for the M1897A4. The gun shield was formed from rolled, face-hardened steel armor, with 0.625-inch plates on the front and 0.25-inch plates on the sides and top. This shield provided protection mainly against splinters. (David Doyle)

The left side of the fighting compartment adjacent to the rear of the 75mm Gun M1897A4 is displayed. The gunner sat in this seat during transit. The seat cover material was water-resistant and it had a zipper for removing a folded blanket roll inside it. (David E. Harper)

At the top of the left side of the fighting compartment to the front of the seat back is a USMC-specific intercom control box with a snap-on canvas cover. The gunner could connect a microphone and earphones to the box to communicate by intercom or radio. (David E. Harper)

The left side of the 75mm gun shield in the background is viewed from the rear of the 75mm Gun M1897A4. A flashlight is on a holder on the side wing of the shield. To the upper right is the perforated shoulder guard to protect the gunner's right shoulder from injury from the recoil of the gun. The gunner's elevating hand wheel is to the far right, below the shoulder guard, and next to it is the traversing hand wheel. (David E. Harper)

The breech of the 75mm Gun M1897A4 is to the upper right, with the firing lanyard hanging from it. At the upper center, a first-aid kit is on the gun shield. Below the gun shield is a sheet-metal box for spare parts for the gun, subsequently fitted with correct lid. (David E. Harper)

The bottom of the 75mm Gun Mount M3 is attached to the carriage support, which includes the two triangular pedestals bolted to the steel plate above the tubes of the 75mm ready-ammunition rack. The steel plate at the top center covers the equilibrators. (David E. Harper)

Under the gun mount are 19 tubes for storing 75mm ammunition. Spring clips held the rounds in place until they were pulled from the tubes. The clips on the two top rows are on the bottoms of the tubes, and the clips for the bottom row are above the tubes. (David Doyle)

The box next to the seat on the right side of the fighting compartment is the gun section chest. It would hold materials and equipment for the maintenance and operation of the gun, from lubricating oil and recoil oil, to tools, to firing lanyard, fuse setter, and spare parts. (David E. Harper)

The gun section chest has a recessed, swiveling ring on the side. A spring clamp fastened to the sponson floor next to the seat is engaged to the ring to secure the chest in place. Two padlock clasps are on the front of the chest lid; hinges are to the rear of the lid. (David E. Harper)

The 75mm Gun M1897A4 is observed through the open rear door of *Tarheel.* The breechblock, of a rotating screw design, is in the open position. It is opened by turning the operating handle counter-clockwise. Attached to the handle is the firing lanyard. (David Doyle)

Here, the breechblock is in the closed position, with the operating handle at about the 4:30 position. The perfectly round, bare metal breechblock fits inside the slightly oblong, olive-drab-painted breech hoop, the swelling at the very rear of the gun. The square plate below the breech is the cover for the equilibrators. The two spring-type equilibrators served to neutralize the unbalanced weight of the 75mm gun and reduced the amount of manual force to elevate the gun. (David E. Harper)

Protruding through an opening at the center top of the covers for the equilibrator is the rear of the elevating arc. The elevating arc, a segment gear with stops at each end to limit maximum elevation and depression, is attached to the bottom of the recoil mechanism. Turning the elevating hand wheels operates an elevation pinion inside the elevating gear case; this pinion acts on the teeth of the elevating arc to move the arc, thus achieving elevation and depression of the gun. (David E. Harper)

With the breechblock in the closed position, the breechblock-operating handle rests at about the 4:30 clock position. The grip of the operating handle is the tube-shaped object extending forward from the outer end of the handle. The lanyard is affixed to a loop on the firing-hammer assembly. To fire the gun, the lanyard was pulled sharply down and to the right and then released, allowing the hammer to strike the firing pin. Also in view is the rear of the elevating arc. (David E. Harper)

The trunnions of the 75mm gun mount provide the lateral pivot points for elevating and depressing the gun. Toward the top center of the photo is the right trunnion. The pin extending from the trunnion was designed for attaching a range quadrant, an instrument used in laying the gun's elevation while conducting indirect fire. However, since the 75mm GMC M3 was configured for direct fire only, the range quadrant was not used. To the right is the right elevating hand wheel. (David E. Harper)

The breechblock is open, with the grip of the operating handle above the breech. The crewman who operated the breechblock was to stand to the right of the breech and grasp the breech-operating handle with his left hand, to avoid injury from the recoiling gun. (David Doyle)

On the right side of the gun carriage is an oval manufacturer's plate. The bottom of the gun shield is cut out to fit around the drum-shaped elevating gear case on the side of the carriage. Between the hand wheel and the carriage is the elevating hand-wheel gear case. (David E. Harper)

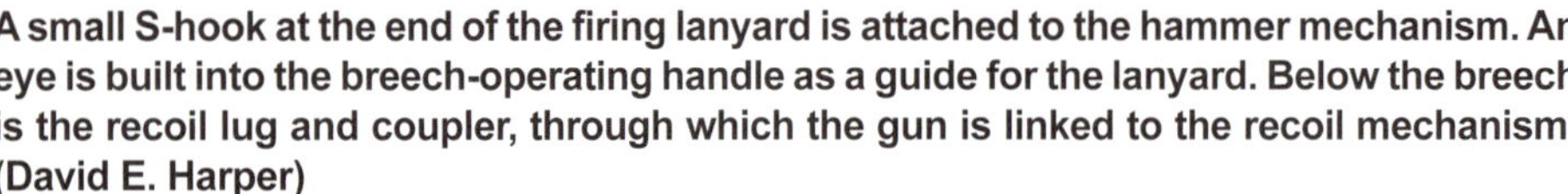

A small S-hook at the end of the firing lanyard is attached to the hammer mechanism. An eye is built into the breech-operating handle as a guide for the lanyard. Below the breech is the recoil lug and coupler, through which the gun is linked to the recoil mechanism. (David E. Harper)

The rear of the 75mm gun mount and the top of the gun shield of *Tarheel* are viewed from the fighting compartment. A brass-colored flashlight is stored in a clip on each side of the shield, and to the left of the gun mount a first-aid kit is fastened to the shield. (David E. Harper)

The gun shield is attached to the gun carriage by a number of braces and fittings. One of the braces is visible below the elevating hand wheel. A clear view is also available of the gun section chest and the manner in which the seat back is mounted on brackets. (David E. Harper)

The top of the gun shield as well as the top of the breech are viewed close-up. A seam running front to rear between the plates of the top of the shield is visible. The ¼-inch armor of the top of the shield provided some overhead protection to the gun crew. (David E. Harper)

In a gunner's-eye view of the 75mm gun mount, the left elevating hand wheel is to the left of the traversing hand wheel. Stamped on the side of the breech is "75 M.M. FIELD GUN / MODEL M1897 / A4." Attached to the left trunnion is a telescopic gun sight. (David E. Harper)

The shoulder guard of the 75mm gun mount includes a rod frame with a perforated piece of sheet metal welded to it. By removing two nuts, the shoulder guard could be removed. To the upper right, details of the firing hammer and lanyard attachment are in view. (David E. Harper)

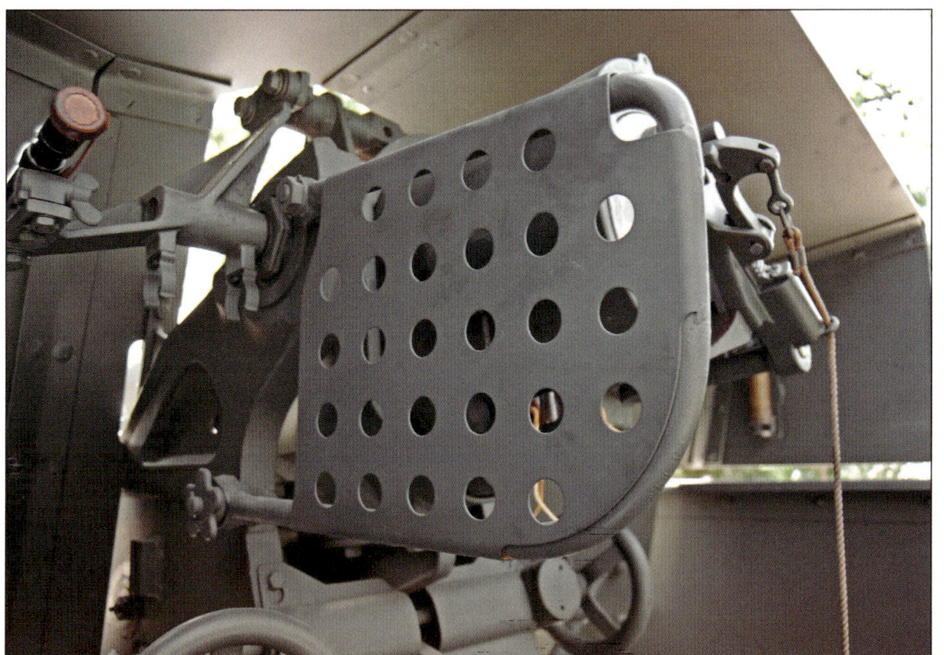

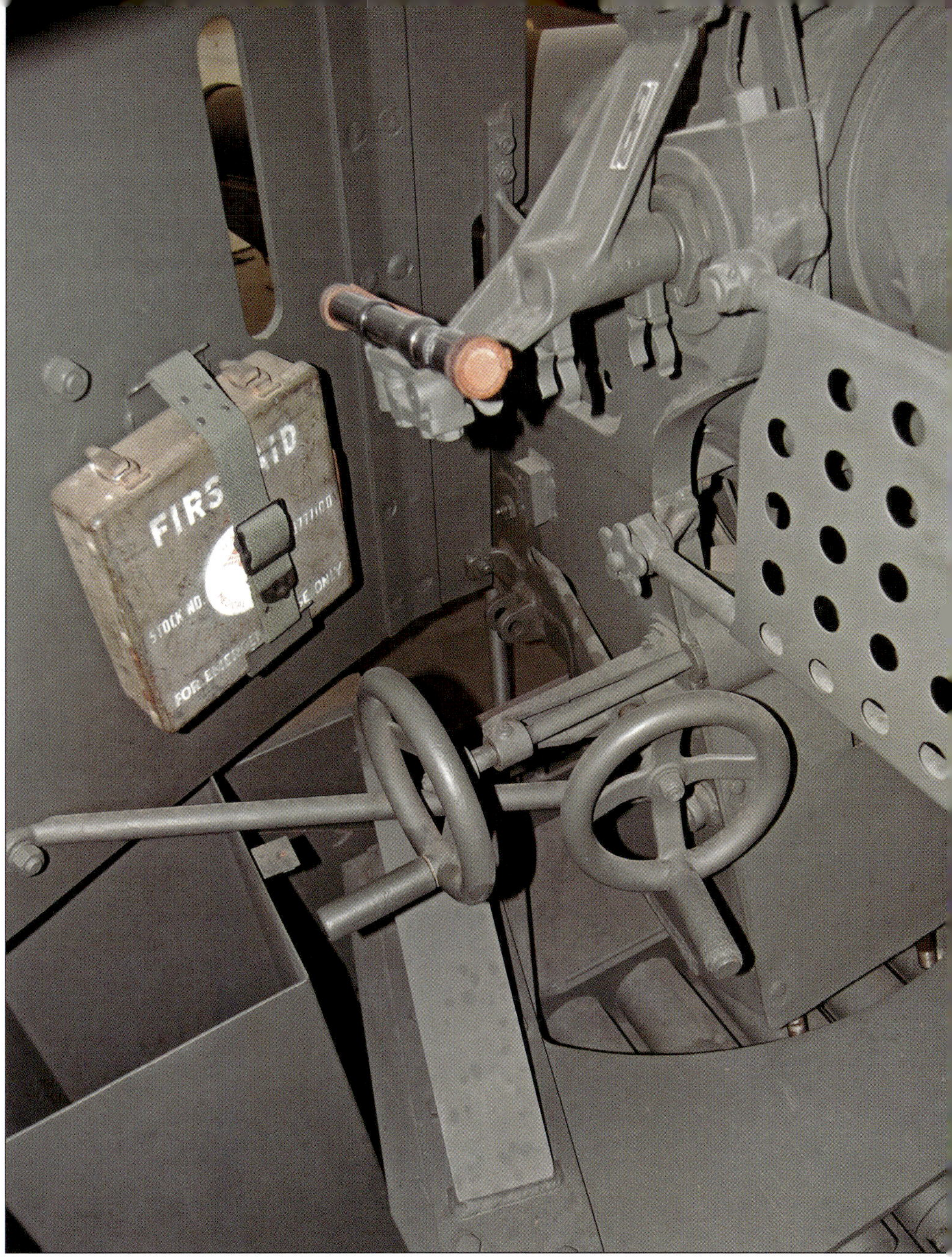

A telescopic gun sight and its mount are attached to the left trunnion. For use on the 75mm GMC M3, the Telescope M33 on the Telescope Mount M36 were specified. This sight was designed for pointing the gun in azimuth and elevation in direct-fire scenarios only. The Telescope Mount M36 was furnished with the Instrument Light M17 to illuminate the telescope reticle for night firing. Telescope covers are fitted on both ends of this telescope. (David E. Harper)

Cut into the gun shield directly to the front of the telescopic sight is a vertical slot through which the telescope would be sighted. Below and to the left of the viewing slot is a first-aid kit, secured to the gun shield with a bracket and a webbing strap with a metal buckle. (David E. Harper)

The gun shield was fabricated from several armor plates. The joints between the plates were strengthened with reinforcing strips, such as the one to the right of the first-aid kit. The front of the shield was specified as 0.625-inch armor; the other plates were 0.25-inch. (David E. Harper)

On the Mount M3, based on the Gun Carriage M2A3, there was an elevating hand wheel (left) and traversing hand wheel (center), and a right elevating hand wheel (far right). Some 75mm GMC M3s had the Mount M5, which lacked the left elevating hand wheel. (David E. Harper)

The underside of the rear of the recoil mechanism is viewed from underneath. Housed in the cradle of the gun, the recoil mechanism has a recoil cylinder to dampen the recoil and a recuperator cylinder to return the gun to its firing position after firing a round. (David E. Harper)

The gunner's hand wheels and the Telescope M33 on the Telescope Mount M36 are displayed. The two clips on the bottom of the telescope mount were for holding a cylindrical-shaped Instrument Light M17 for illuminating the telescope's reticule. (David Doyle)

Leather covers are fitted over the front and the rear of the telescope. The large wing nut on the telescope mount below the rear of the telescope is a locking cam, for locking the rear of the telescope in place. The mount was adjustable for elevation and deflection. (David E. Harper)

The Telescope M33 and the Telescope Mount M36 are viewed from another angle. The telescope was a one-power telescope with a field of view of 11 degrees. A rubber eye shield and a rubber shield for the objective of the telescope were available. Part of the upper portion of the gun shield is viewed from the gunner's perspective. The plates of the shield are joined together with flat and angled steel straps. (David E. Harper)

The traversing hand wheel, bottom, is connected to a shaft which proceeds forward into a slot in the lower part of the left side of the 75mm gun carriage, and then on to the traversing gear. The traversing mechanism of the Gun Mount M3 could traverse the 75mm gun a total of 40 degrees: 19 degrees to the left and 21 degrees to the right. (David E. Harper)

As seen from the 75mm gunner's perspective looking through the gap between the left pedestal of the gun mount (left) and the left side of the gun carriage (right), several of the tubes of the 75mm ready-ammunition rack below the gun mount are visible below the center of the photo. The horizontal tube in the background is part of the carriage support. (David E. Harper)

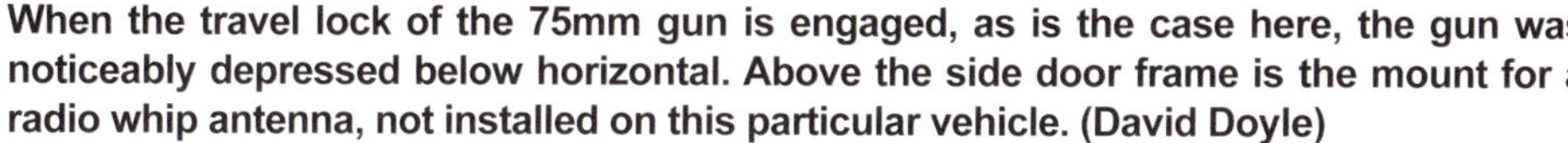

When the travel lock of the 75mm gun is engaged, as is the case here, the gun was noticeably depressed below horizontal. Above the side door frame is the mount for a radio whip antenna, not installed on this particular vehicle. (David Doyle)

The right tracked suspension is the mirror image of that on the left side of the 75mm GMC M3. The tailpipe of the engine exhaust is to the immediate front of the track-support roller. A mold seam is visible all along the edge of the rubber track. (David E. Harper)

The rubber seam along the center of the edge of the track is viewed from a closer perspective. The projections along the edge of the track indicate where the steel crossbars are located inside the rubber-encased tracks. These projections aided traction. (David E. Harper)

Some of the treads at the upper rear of the right track are displayed. As part of the process of molding rubber around the steel cables and crossbars that form the guts of the tracks, small rubber sprues are left at each corner of each tread; most of these are still present. (David E. Harper)

The B. F. Goodrich logotype is visible on the side of the rubber tire of the right rear bogie roller. The movement of the rubber tires on rubber tracks made for a smoother ride as well as a quieter one, lessening the chance alerting the enemy to the vehicle's approach. (David E. Harper)

The rear arms of the crab of the right bogie assembly project from the bogie frame and rest on pads built into the tops of the bogie arms. The two rear bogie rollers ride in a frame, the center of which swivels on the ends of the bogie arms via a spindle. (David E. Harper)

When adjusting track tension, the vehicle ideally was preloaded to its operating weight, and the idler wheel was adjusted rearward until, with a man of average weight standing on the track between the idler wheel and the track-support roller, it had $\frac{3}{4}$-inch sag. (David E. Harper)

Both arms of the outboard side of the crab of the right bogie assembly are visible. Upside-down casting numbers are present toward the end of each arm of the crab. The outer face of the bogie frame to the left of center of the photo has a rough texture. (David E. Harper)

As seen on the right drive sprocket assembly of *Tarheel,* the sprocket itself is sandwiched between two flanges reinforced with spokes and perforated with numerous lightening holes. Also in view is the tail pipe as it bends under the chassis frame. (David E. Harper)

Projecting from underneath the right side of the cab between the small running board and the fender is the battery box. The box held a six-cell, 12-volt battery; the type specified was the Willard Model WH-25-6. The armored top and side of the box were removable. (David E. Harper)

As viewed from below the right side of the cab of *Tarheel* facing aft, in the foreground is the rear axle and differential. This differential, which drives the tracks, has a gear ratio of 4.44:1. The axle is connected by a drive shaft to the transfer case at the far right. (David E. Harper)

More details of the rear axle and differential and the drive shaft are available. The gray transfer case is to the top right. The brake drums were made of gun iron with high wear resistance. The brakes were conventional hydraulic, two-shoe, internal-expanding type. (David E. Harper)

Looking underneath the cab from the right side to the left, the transfer case is at the center. It transfers power from the transmission to the drive shafts, including one powering the front axle in the foreground, and one powering the rear axle to the left. (David E. Harper)

Between the transfer case and the drive shaft is the disk of the Tru-Stop two-shoe ventilated drive-shaft brake. The green mechanism to the left of the brake disk is the brake mechanism, including two brake shoes, operated by a lever in the cab. (David E. Harper)

The rear drive shaft is viewed from a closer perspective, with the transfer case and Tru-Stop drive-shaft brake by American Cable Co. to the left and the rear axle to the right. A universal joint is on each end of the drive shaft. Opposite the drive shaft is the muffler. (David E. Harper)

To the left, mounted under the left side of the cab, is the vacuum booster of the hydraulic brake system. It was specified as manufactured by Bragg-Kleiserath and was a poppet-valve, reactionary-cylinder, puller-type unit. To the lower right is the transfer case. (David E. Harper)

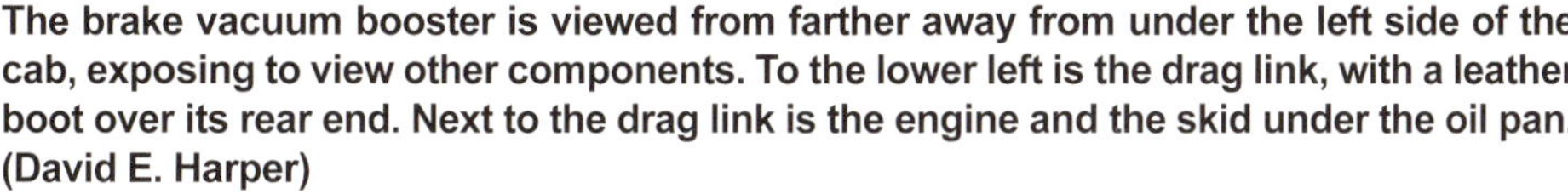

The brake vacuum booster is viewed from farther away from under the left side of the cab, exposing to view other components. To the lower left is the drag link, with a leather boot over its rear end. Next to the drag link is the engine and the skid under the oil pan. (David E. Harper)

The oil pan of the engine and its protective skid with an access hole in the bottom for the drain plug are observed from the right side. Also in view are the front axle, differential, and leaf springs and angled extensions of the armor that protects the oil pan. (David E. Harper)

The transmission (upper right) is the Spicer 3461, a constant-mesh type with four forward speeds and one reverse. Elements of the steering system are in view, including the drag link, the steering gear above the drag link, and the tie rod aft of the front axle. (David E. Harper)

To the right of the cab, the battery box has a removable top plate and side plate, secured by hex screws, for accessing the battery. Stored in two brackets above the battery box and secured with a leather strap is an axe. The small running board has diamond tread. (David E. Harper)

Tarheel is viewed from the right side, the 75mm Gun M1897A4 slightly depressed, as the travel lock is engaged to it. Below the barrel of the 75mm gun is the cradle, the bottom of which has a distinctive V shape as viewed from the front or rear. The cradle houses the recoil mechanism of the gun, including the recoil cylinder and recuperator, hidden inside the cradle. The gun-slide bearing is the brass-colored structure protruding from the front of the cradle. (David Doyle)

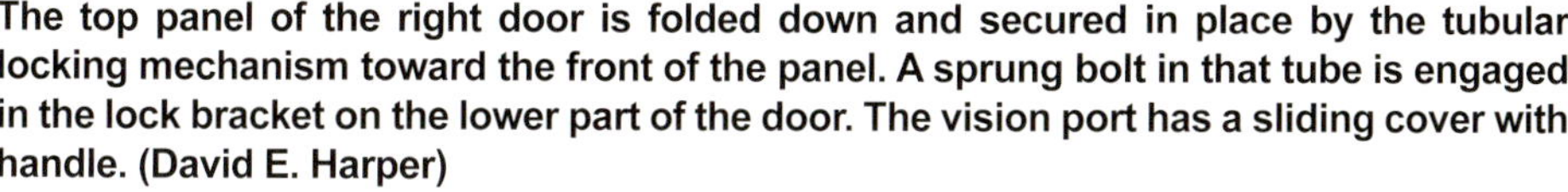

The top panel of the right door is folded down and secured in place by the tubular locking mechanism toward the front of the panel. A sprung bolt in that tube is engaged in the lock bracket on the lower part of the door. The vision port has a sliding cover with handle. (David E. Harper)

A holder for a lubrication chart is on the inside of the right door. To the left of the chart holder is the holder assembly, for securing the top plate of the door in the raised position. To the right of the chart holder are the door handle and lock and a sliding-bolt latch. (David E. Harper)

The cab is viewed through the open right door. The closer seat was that assigned to the assistant driver, who also served as the radio operator in vehicles so equipped. Next to the seat are the A-frame-type travel lock of the gun and the radio rack with canvas cover. (David E. Harper)

The assistant driver's seat is viewed from overhead, with the 75mm gun shield to the bottom of the photo and the radio antenna mount on the top of the door frame to the right. The floor of the cab has diamond tread. To the far left is the barrel of the 75mm gun. (David E. Harper)

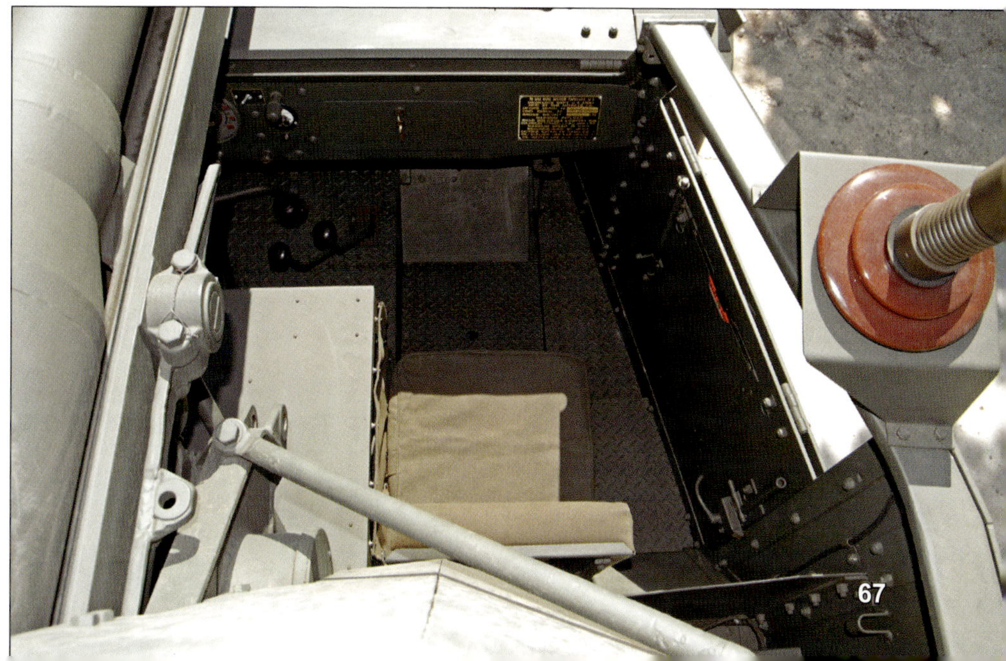

Antenna mounts for the 75mm GMC M3 came in several different designs and locations. The one on *Tarheel* is located on top of the frame over the right door of the cab. The antenna mount is attached to a bracket, with a reddish insulator at the base of the mount. (David E. Harper)

The antenna mount is viewed facing toward the rear. Under the top of the mounting bracket is the electrical connection for the antenna, with a cable attached to it. The antenna mount incorporates a steel spring that allows for the antenna's flexibility. (David E. Harper)

The antenna mount is observed from the right side of the cab facing slightly upward. The bracket for the antenna mount was fabricated from bent sheet metal. Also in view is the right side of the 75mm gun shield, including a brace bolted to the shield and the carriage. (David E. Harper)

The right side of the 75mm gun shield is viewed from slightly to the rear, showing the relative position of the shield and the radio antenna mount. The slotted, oval-headed screws toward the top of the body of the vehicle fasten the sill to the inside of the body. (David E. Harper)

The travel lock is latched to a fitting on the bottom of the gun cradle. The bottoms of the two legs of the travel lock are in swivel mounts below the front of the gun carriage. Deploying the travel lock helped prevent damage to the elevating gears during transit. (David E. Harper)

The travel lock swivels in brackets welded to the support structure of the gun mount. Above the travel lock is the traversing rack, above which is the traversing gear case, at the bottom of which is a pinion that turns against the traversing rack to traverse the gun. (David E. Harper)

Like the other seats in the 75mm GMC M3, the assistant driver's seat has a cushioned bottom and back. The cushions comprised water-resistant covers fitted with zippers for removing the folded blankets within. The frame of the seat back is hinged to enable lowering the seat back if desired. Next to the assistant driver's seat is the radio rack. (David E. Harper)

The radio rack between the seats in the cab has a canvas dust cover, secured in place with snaps. The equipment inside the rack was accessible from the assistant driver's side, as he also functioned as the radio operator. The bottom of the rack is raised off the floor. (David E. Harper)

Radio equipment in the rack is visible with the cover partially detached. The components in the rack at the time it was photographed were Naval-aviation types. The component to the front of the rack has an antenna current meter and thus probably is a transmitter. (David E. Harper)

The lever to the front of the assistant driver's seat controls the opening and shutting of the armored louvers in front of the radiator. The upper part of the lever is within a retainer bracket, and an operating rod is linked to the lower part of the lever. Affixed to the dashboard is a data plate listing the vehicle's nomenclature ("75 MM. Gun, Motor Carriage, M-3"), manufacturer (Autocar Co.), manufacturer's serial number (M3-75-1939), ordnance serial number (1939), and selected capacities and specifications. (David E. Harper)

With the driver's side door open, the driver's seat, steering wheel, instrument panel, and control levers are in view. The seat cushion rests in a seat pan fastened to the floor. A webbing thong fastened to the zipper of the seat-cushion cover lies to the side of the seat. A U-bolt holds the steering column to a bracket below the dashboard. The black object fastened to the door frame is a compass. Below the door are pioneer tools. In the background is the 75mm gun, with the gun cradle being particularly prominent. (David E. Harper)

The lone instrument to the far left of the dashboard is the tachometer, with a scale up to 3,500 rpm. The placard to the left of the tachometer cautions against operating the engine over 2,000 rpm until the cooling system temperature has reached 160 degrees. (David E. Harper)

As viewed from the driver's position in the cab, nestled in the front of the gun carriage and to the rear of the travel lock is the traversing gear case, below which is a pinion that turns in mesh with the traversing rack to effect the traversing of the gun mount. (David E. Harper)

The traversing rack is fixed to the support of the gun mount, while the traversing gear case and the pinion attached to the bottom of it are secured to the gun carriage. The tubular-shaped structure below the carriage is part of the gun-mount support. (David E. Harper)

With the back of the driver's seat folded forward, details of the bulkhead and gun mount to the rear are visible. The cushion of the seat is attached to a sheet-metal seat back, which in turn is fastened to two vertical frames, each of which is hinged at the bottom. (David E. Harper)

The driver's seat is viewed with the seat back in the normal, raised position. When the 75mm GMC M3 deployed for combat, training doctrine called for the driver and the assistant driver to lower the armored windshield cover and crouch down in their seats while the gun crew went into action. In photos of the M3 during combat, the driver's door often is seen open or partially open. (David E. Harper)

As viewed from the left rear of the 75mm gun shield, mounted at the top front of the left door frame is the driver's rear-view mirror – a feature not found on M3 Personnel Carriers or M2 half tracks. The armored windshield cover is lowered onto the hood. To the right, the widest part of the gun barrel is called the jacket.

The full extent of the transmission shift lever is displayed. This lever has a broad curve in it to provide clearance for the parking brake lever. On the right side of the transmission shift lever are the transfer-case shift lever and the front-wheel-drive shift lever. (David E. Harper)

Flanking the steering column are the clutch pedal (left) and the brake pedal (right). The accelerator pedal is to the right of the brake pedal. Below the steering column is the dimmer switch. To the right are the transmission shift lever and the parking brake lever. (David E. Harper)

The black selector switch on the dashboard to the front of the steering wheel is the electric brake load control, a rheostat for adjusting for heavy, medium, and light loads. The olive drab controls above it are the panel light control and the main light switch. (David Doyle)

The horn button on the steering wheel has a "Ross Cam & Lever Steering" logo, a reference to the Ross Model TA26 cam and twin lever steering gear. The large gauge under glass to the right of the upper spoke of the steering wheel is the instrument cluster. (David E. Harper)

The interior of the driver's door is similar to that of the assistant driver's door, except that the driver's door lacks a holder for a lubrication chart. It has the holder assembly for the top plate of the door, the door handle and lock, a sliding-bolt latch, and two small D-rings. (David E. Harper)

Below the tachometer on the left side of the dashboard is a placard, brass with black paint, with operating instructions for, left to right, the transmission shift lever, the hand brake, the transfer case shift lever, and the front-wheel-drive shift lever. (David E. Harper)

The driver's rear view mirror is viewed from the exterior of the vehicle facing upward and forward, with the top of the door frame and, to the right, the upper front corner of the side of the fighting compartment in view. The mirror strut is adjustable for length. (David E. Harper)

On a holder mounted on the cowl to the front of the assistant driver's door is stored a five-gallon liquid container. The five-gallon containers on each side of the cowl of *Tarheel* are in addition to the two five-gallon liquid containers stored in the fighting compartment. At the bottom is the battery box. (David E. Harper)

The five-gallon liquid container stored on the right side of the cowl of *Tarheel* is viewed facing toward the rear, also showing the liquid container's holder and its mounting bracket, the lowered armored windshield cover, the battery box, and the right door. To the far right is the rear clamp of the hood. (David E. Harper)

With the right side of the hood open, the rear of the engine compartment is in view. The black object is the air cleaner, on top of which are the horn (not to be confused with the warning device) and a flexible air hose. The air cleaner, which filtered all air entering the carburetor, was the oil-bath type, and it was fitted with a breather tube that conducted fumes from the crankcase to the carburetor. (David E. Harper)

In a view of the right side of the engine compartment, the carburetor is above the center of the exhaust manifold. The specified carburetor was the Stromberg Model 380053, a duplex downdraft aero type. The pipe with the reddish-orange cap is the oil-filler tube. (David E. Harper)

The carburetor is mounted to a flange on top of the intake manifold, most of which is hidden below the exhaust manifold. The black canister toward the right, aft of the radiator, is the oil filter; the type specified was DeLuxe Products Corp. Model CS-602W. (David E. Harper)

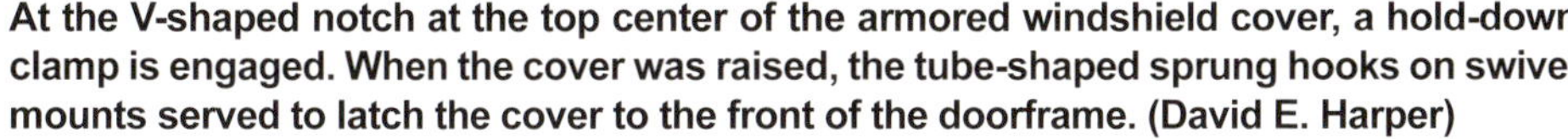
At the V-shaped notch at the top center of the armored windshield cover, a hold-down clamp is engaged. When the cover was raised, the tube-shaped sprung hooks on swivel mounts served to latch the cover to the front of the doorframe. (David E. Harper)

Three ring-shaped supports secure the barrel of the 75mm gun to the slide bearings below the barrel, which guide the gun during recoil and recuperation. From front to rear, they are designated the muzzle support, the intermediate support, and the jacket support. (David E. Harper)

The muzzle of the 75mm Gun M1897A5 has various markings stamped on its face. A frontal view of the gun's slide assembly, at the top of the gun cradle and recoil mechanism, is available. Tilted braces are attached from the carriage to the gun shield. (David E. Harper)

Small thumbscrews at the upper center of each vision port on the windshield cover held the sliding covers of the ports in the open position. The two nuts and bolts to each side of the ports were for fastening the guides for the covers of the ports. (David E. Harper)

On the right fender are two sets of footman loops and webbing straps with buckles for securing a tarpaulin, canvas cover, camouflage netting, or other equipment. Both handles on the side of the hood are visible. To the upper right on top of the fender is the early-type, large, non-removable service headlight assembly with separate blackout marker lamp and a large brush guard. (David E. Harper)

The right service headlight, blackout marker lamp, and brush guard are viewed from the front. The brush guard consists of rod crosspieces, the vertical ones split so the horizontal ones pass through them, fitted to a welded frame attached to mounting brackets. (David E. Harper)

The underside of the right fender is viewed from behind the tire (visible at the top right), facing upward, showing the rear fender support, welded from channel sections. The flange on the inboard side of the fender is bolted to the armored body of the vehicle. (David E. Harper)

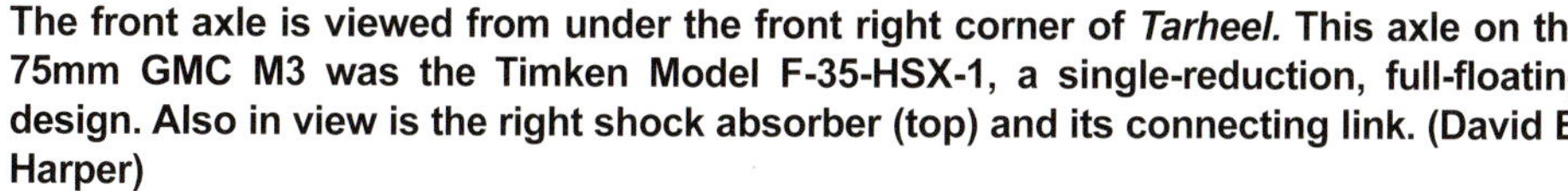

The front axle is viewed from under the front right corner of *Tarheel.* This axle on the 75mm GMC M3 was the Timken Model F-35-HSX-1, a single-reduction, full-floating design. Also in view is the right shock absorber (top) and its connecting link. (David E. Harper)

The front bumper roller helps the vehicle to maneuver over ditches and holes. It is mounted on brackets with coil compression springs to absorb the shock when the roller hit an obstruction. On the fender is the UNIS code for Weapons Company, 28th Marines. (David E. Harper)

The front axle is observed from the left side. A drain plug is present on the front of the differential. A curved guard on each side of the axle served to protect the steering knuckles from damage. The engine oil pan and its protective skid are aft of the axle. (David E. Harper)

Below and aft of the bumper is a curved extension of the frontal armor to protect the bottom of the radiator. Three steel reinforcing straps are fastened to the bumper and to the bottom of the armor extension. The front hanger of the right leaf spring is visible. (David E. Harper)

The restored M3 Gun Motor Carriage, with Veteran M3 crewman Hank Backlund at the wheel, moves across a faux battlefield during a reenactment. The M3 was one of many specialized vehicles created on the White-designed halftrack chassis. Most, like the M3, were replaced with fully tracked vehicles which provided greater mobility as well as more extensive armor protect for the crew. Nonetheless, the M3 proved an able vehicle filling an immediate need in Italy, North Africa, and the Pacific. (David Doyle)